T0098605

ABOVE THE LAW

ABOVE THE LAW

HOW "QUALIFIED IMMUNITY" PROTECTS VIOLENT POLICE

BEN COHEN

WITH A FOREWORD BY MICHAEL RENDER ("KILLER MIKE")

O/R

OR Books

New York · London

© 2021 Ben Cohen

Published by OR Books, New York and London
Visit our website at www.orbooks.com

All rights information: rights@orbooks.com

First printing 2021

Library of Congress Cataloging-in-Publication Data: A catalog record for this book is available from the Library of Congress.
British Library Cataloging in Publication Data: A catalog record for this book is available from the British Library.

Typeset by Lapiz Digital.

paperback ISBN 978-1-68219-257-3 • ebook ISBN 978-1-68219-265-8

CONTENTS

FOREWORD

*Not everything that is faced can be changed, but nothing
can be changed until it is faced.*

—James Baldwin

On the night of May 30, 2020, I was standing at the Mayor
of Atlanta's podium, wondering what I might say to keep
my hometown from burning itself to the ground before
the sun came up in the morning.

The fury erupting in the streets of Atlanta in George
Floyd's name that night was the cry of generations, and
it was a righteous cry, and it was justified. Standing there
before those TV cameras, I thought of Mr. Floyd in his last
moments on Earth, his neck crushed under the knee of a
cop who once took an oath to serve and protect his community, his partner standing watch while Mr. Floyd cried
out for his mother in heaven and died.

I thought of the next generation of Black boys and girls
across America who watched that horrible lynching on

their phones and I wondered how many of them were no longer surprised by what they saw. I wondered how many would go on themselves to die at the hands of a racist law enforcement system not far removed from slave patrols of the antebellum South or the decades of Jim Crow oppression that haunted my people afterward. I felt the old rage rising in my own heart and burning in my own eyes, too.

Looking back on that night, I know that a part of me wanted to watch the world burn, as well. A part of me wondered if it wouldn't be better than the alternative, of living in a world like this one, where every day it seems I am waking up to watch another Black person die.

At the same time, I knew burning ourselves down was not the way. Atlanta is the homeland. Atlanta is to the Black diaspora, in my mind, every bit as significant as Israel is to the Jewish community, as Brazil is to the Pan-African community. One hundred and twenty years of economic opportunity for Black Americans like my grandmother, who moved here in 1952, or my grandfather, who arrived ten years earlier. Fifty years of Black mayoral leadership. A city that is thriving, even if it ain't perfect. A city with the third-most Fortune 500 companies in the nation. A city home to the "Atlanta Conference of Negro Problems," hosted by Booker T. Washington and W.E.B. Du Bois each year from 1896 to 1914. A city where more than fifty restaurants are now owned by Black people, and in particular

Black women. Atlanta could not fall, not like this, not right now. We had to fortify.

I was duty-bound to speak directly to Atlanta at that moment—to remind everyone, including myself, that we must remain a fortress in a sea of chaos. We do not have to destroy our homes, our neighborhoods, our businesses. We do not have to give in to despair the way they want us to. We do not have to live our lives in grief and anguish that spans the days between one martyred hashtag and the next. We do not have to hang our hopes on some damn prosecutor to "do the right thing" after they stood by and let the wrong thing happen, again and again.

So I swallowed down my anger, and I opened my remarks by laying down the truest line I knew: "I didn't want to come," I said. "And I don't want to be here."

First, before we talk about qualified immunity, let me say something about cops that needs to be said. I am the proud son of a former officer of the Atlanta Police Department. Two of my cousins are police officers right now. Based on what I experienced growing up here in Atlanta, I believe that there are cops who are not inherently bad or evil people, who want to keep our communities safe and who work hard to do so. One example right off the bat is Officer Tommy Norman out in North Little Rock, a guy I've thrown some shine to before on my podcast. Maybe you've seen Tommy on his social media accounts—if not, look him up sometime. Tommy doesn't live in his patrol car, looking to hit some arrest quota by the end of the month. He *knows* the people on his beat, and they know him back. North Little Rock ain't an easy place to be a cop, but even still, people in the community don't fear for their lives the second they see Tommy's squad car roll up. That's a testament to him. That's because he does it *right*.

With that said, even good cops like Tommy Norman still operate inside a larger system *that is itself* overly militarized, harshly punitive (particularly against Black Americans), and absent of any real legal accountability—as we continue to see, time and time again, with these cops who murder my people with impunity. As a result, bad cops are allowed to make good cops like Tommy's jobs even harder, because of the public trust that has been broken. And there will be no fixing that public trust—or the law enforcement system as a whole—without first ending the legal doctrine known as qualified immunity.

Qualified immunity is the rule that protects government employees from being taken to task for assaults on your constitutional rights—in this instance, your Eighth Amendment right against cruel and unusual punishment at the hands of the state—so long as those employees did not violate "<u>clearly established</u>" law. Of all the predatory elements of American policing (and there are many, from the legal chokeholds to monthly arrest quotas to the NYPD's infamous stop-and-frisk policy) the qualified immunity doctrine is perhaps the single lynchpin that holds the entire machine together. Without ending qualified immunity, there's no way to hold bad cops accountable for their violent crimes against the American people. The system will perpetuate itself largely undisturbed, the violence will rage on and on, and Black communities all over the country will keep on living in fear of the very people sworn allegedly to protect them.

The goal of a democratic society is to create and protect a system of government where all people, no matter their race, class, religion, gender, sexuality, or creed, are treated fairly and with human dignity. I would not say it is highly disputable that our country has not yet achieved that goal, no matter what patriotic stuff our politicians tell us every two to four years. But if we as Americans are going to take a good-faith approach toward *attempting* to achieve that goal, one area where we must begin is in fixing our broken and brutal law enforcement system. This starts with ending qualified immunity.

The progression of law enforcement in America through the centuries has been a shameful story of racism and oppression. You don't need to take my word on that—I'll leave it to the top law-and-order experts themselves. As recently as 2018, one of Donald Trump's former

Attorneys General, good old Jeff Sessions of Alabama, said to a roomful of white cops at the National Sheriff's Association winter conference that the office of the sheriff was "a critical part of the *Anglo-American heritage* of law enforcement." Now, Jeff was honest in saying that, but sadly it was just a very nice, very professional way of saying that sheriff's departments began as slave-catcher organizations and have not come very far in the centuries since. And they haven't.

We have to be honest with ourselves about how law enforcement has taken hold in American society. What began as a slave-catcher's role eventually evolved into, after the Thirteenth Amendment technically abolished chattel slavery, an agent of legally imposed Jim Crow oppression on Black Americans. As the decades went on and various important civil rights victories were achieved, police departments got more creative. They began the practice we see today of hiring people who *look like* the oppressed groups, but are still forced to do the bidding of a prison industrial system that perpetuates those groups' oppression each and every day.

What does that system look like now? It's a system where a Black person is five times more likely to be stopped by police without just cause than a white person. It's a system where between 900 and 1,100 people are shot and killed by police each year—with much higher proportions in the Black community, when accounting for total population. The United States is not first place in that many categories today, but our law enforcement system does lead the developed world in terms of body count. In fact, we blow other nations out of the water. It ain't even a competition. How many people do cops kill annually in Canada? Thirty-six. In France? Twenty-six. In Australia? Four. In Denmark, Iceland, and Switzerland combined? They kill zero people.

Not surprisingly, it turns out that when a nation equips its police departments with the gear, weaponry, and authoritarian mindset of occupying armies, those departments come to see their communities as enemy combatants, and the streets of America as a war zone. The doctrine of qualified immunity for police officers more or less guarantees this will continue to be the case, no matter what other reforms we try to pass at the state or federal level.

As the calls to prosecute Officer Derek Chauvin grew louder in the days following Mr. Floyd's murder in Minneapolis—calls which I *agreed* with—I couldn't help but think of the futility of the effort in the end. Prosecution was not going to bring that man back from the dead. Prosecution is not going to bring Breonna Taylor back, or Tamir Rice or Renisha McBride or Eric Garner or Rekia Boyd or Philando Castile or Natasha McKenna or Michael Brown or anyone. Prosecution is a hollow victory for communities racked by generations of torment and rage. Prosecution does not excuse the system that created the murderer and their victim, the master and his slave, the occupier and the occupied. Anybody can do the right thing after the wrong thing has happened. Anybody can punish individuals after the fact. But what does that do for the next victim? What does that do for the next Black family in America who will lose their child or father or mother to martyrdom and does not know it yet? Legal actions that don't change the mechanics of the system are empty concessions to disguise what those mechanics are all about. Policing in America today is born out of the nucleus of authoritarianism, the mindset of: "I can kill you, no matter the reason, and nothing will happen to me." As organizers and activists, we have got to go further than simply seeking punishment for individual officers after they have ended a life. We have to change the culture of policing itself, to *save the next life*. We have to end qualified immunity.

The most important thing I have learned through my life and career is that evil does not care who it collaborates with. Evil cooperates better than good. Evil will collaborate with somebody good so long as it will meet the ends of evil. What this means is that good people, people married to principle and morals and a vision for a better world, *have* to start looking past our differences. If not, we are always going to always lose against evil.

Sometimes the fight against evil feels heavy and hopeless. But it's not hopeless. ***Plot, plan, strategize, organize, and mobilize.*** You start by yourself. You plot out what you want to see in the world, you maybe do a little planning by yourself. But then you begin to strategize with the others around you—in your building, on your street, in your office. And then you organize with others. And then, finally, you mobilize together. In that struggle, we discover solidarity with other human beings—and that is something that no evil can take from us.

The book in your hands is an effort to mobilize together.

It is not as lonely when you understand you ain't alone.

Michael Render
"Killer Mike"

PREFACE

Countless people have been victimized by police misconduct. They have lost loved ones, suffered traumatic and debilitating injuries, or had their property damaged, destroyed, or stolen.

This book tells the true stories of a few of the people who have suffered the dual injustice of police misconduct and qualified immunity. It also includes short articles about qualified immunity from police officers, judges, lawyers, activists, and constitutional experts. We hope that it will inform you about this issue and inspire you to take action.

All royalties from this book go to the Campaign to End Qualified Immunity. To learn more or to make a donation, visit our website at campaigntoendqualifiedimmunity.org.

SONIA SOTOMAYOR

"As I have previously noted, this Court routinely displays an unflinching willingness "to summarily reverse courts for wrongly denying officers the protection of qualified immunity" but "rarely intervene[s] where courts wrongly afford officers the benefit of qualified immunity in these same cases."[1] **Such a one-sided approach to qualified immunity transforms the doctrine into an absolute shield for law enforcement officers**, gutting the deterrent effect of the Fourth Amendment.

The majority today exacerbates that troubling asymmetry. Its decision is not just wrong on the law; it also sends an alarming signal to law enforcement officers and

---

1 [Id., at ___–___ (slip op., at 8–9); see also Baude, Is Qualified Immunity Unlawful? 106 Cal. L. Rev. 45, 82 (2018) ("[N]early all of the Supreme Court's qualified immunity cases come out the same way—by finding immunity for the officials"); Reinhardt, The Demise of Habeas Corpus and the Rise of Qualified Immunity: The Court's Ever Increasing Limitations on the Development Cite as: 584 U. S. ___ (2018) 15 SOTOMAYOR, J., dissenting and Enforcement of Constitutional Rights and Some Particularly Unfortunate Consequences, 113 Mich. L. Rev. 1219, 1244–1250 (2015).

the public. It tells officers that they can shoot first and think later, and it tells the public that palpably unreasonable conduct will go unpunished. Because there is nothing right or just under the law about this, I respectfully dissent."

—*Kisela v. Hughes*, U.S. Supreme Court Justice
Sonia Sotomayor, dissenting

WALKING WHILE BLACK

In the summer of 2016, David Collie worked full-time building produce displays for supermarkets in Fort Worth, Texas. He was saving up to return to college that fall. On the night of July 27, David went to visit some friends who lived nearby. He wanted to check in and say hello to their kids. They called him "Uncle David."

Meanwhile, two off-duty police officers heard a radio description of two suspects in a nearby robbery. The dispatcher described the suspects: Black males in their teens or early twenties, one with a height of six foot one, the other, six foot four. The suspects, one apparently armed with a small pistol, stole two pairs of sneakers after arranging a deal on Facebook.

The cops saw David—five foot six and thirty-three years old (at least seven inches shorter and ten years older) but Black—walking into his friends' apartment complex. They shouted at him from their unmarked car as he continued to walk toward his friends' apartment. But David didn't know what they wanted. Did they want to see his hands? Did they want to know where he was going? "I was trying to comply," David recalled. "I did hear him say 'take your hand out of your pocket,'" David told a reporter a few months later. "So in my mind, I'm, like, trying to be like, 'look, I'm showing my hand.'"

David took his hand out of his pocket, raised his right arm, and pointed away from the cops, toward the nearest building, where he was headed. That's when one cop, standing thirty-four feet away, opened fire, and shot David in the back, severing his spine.

Approximately five seconds passed between the beginning of the encounter and when the officer fired his weapon.

David fell to the pavement and cried out, "You didn't have to shoot me!"

In the hospital, he was handcuffed to his bed. Paralyzed from the waist down and suffering from a collapsed lung, David spent the next two months in the hospital fighting false charges that he assaulted the officer. They were "painting a dirty picture," David told a reporter a few months after the shooting. "It's not the truth."

The charges *were* untrue. The police officers falsified police reports to try to protect themselves.

David's lawyer called the charges "revolting and repugnant." It was the police, he argued, who were breaking the law by compounding their attacks on David. "It's a crime to falsify police reports, to say that someone lunged at you, or pointed a weapon at you. It's a crime to shoot someone in the back from thirty-four feet away."

The police closed ranks around their officers. The officer who shot David was put on paid leave while police conducted an internal investigation that their spokesperson said lasted just "a few days."

After stalling for a Freedom of Information Act request, the district attorney's office shared dashcam footage of the shooting with David's attorney. The video clearly shows that David was never anywhere near the officers, much less assaulting them. The cop's body cam, which might have yielded a clearer picture of the incident, had conveniently cut out before he exited his cruiser, and did not resume capturing video until after the shooting.

Despite the damages, the months in the hospital, and enduring vindictive charges and police stonewalling, David didn't give up. He sued the police and the officers in federal court.

The police benefited from taxpayer-funded lawyers who fought hard for qualified immunity. The lawyers argued that the officers had acted reasonably because they feared for their safety. They emphasized that one of the robbery suspects was armed and pointed to the dashcam footage, which shows David raising his arm to the side while walking away from the officers.

The court sided with the police, granting them qualified immunity. They concluded that there "is no doubt that innocent citizens have a clearly established right not to be shot by police officers," but that David could not sue because "reasonable officers could differ on the lawfulness of" the officer's decision to shoot.

Going on little more than the officers' statements about what they felt, the judges denied David justice and ruled that the cops' decision to shoot him was "objectively reasonable."

Now thirty-seven, David lives in an assisted-living facility, sharing a bathroom with another resident. He struggles to get by on Social Security and Medicaid.

"Paralyzed over some tennis shoes?" David laments. "Come on, man. You're playing with a human life here."

Had he prevailed in court, David might have been able to afford to renovate his mother's house to enable wheelchair access. He holds out hope that he will one day be able to live with his family, but he is aware of what he has lost: his mobility, his job, his dream of being a cinematographer.

***

References

1. *Collie v. Baron, et al* (Opinion, Northern Dist. of Texas).
2. Andrew Chung, Lawrence Hurley, Andrea Januta, Jackie Botts, and Jaimi Dowdell, "Shot by cops, thwarted

by judges and geography." *Reuters* (Aug. 25, 2020).
https://www.reuters.com/investigates/special-report/
usa-police-immunity-variations/

3. *Collie v. Baron* (Per Curiam Opinion, 5th Circuit Court of
Appeals, 2018).

4. *Valdez v. MacDonald, et al* (District Court of Colorado; order
denying QI).

5. Jack Fink, "Now Paralyzed, Fort Worth Man Shot By Police
Speaks Out For First Time." *CBS DFW* (February 14, 2017).
https://dfw.cbslocal.com/2017/02/14/now-paralyzed-fort-
worth-man-shot-by-police-speaks-out-for-first-time/.

6. Scott Gordon and Cory Minderhout, "Man Paralyzed After
Being Shot in His Back by Fort Worth Police: Lawyer." *CBS
DFW* (December 27, 2016). https://www.nbcdfw.com/news/
local/fort-worth-officer-involved-shooting-video-released-
by-law-firm/201109/.

7. David Warren, "Video appears to show Texas police shooting
man walking away." *Star Tribune* (December 28, 2016).
https://www.startribune.com/video-appears-to-show-
texas-police-shooting-man-walking-away/408515215/.

8. Kevin Conlon and Steve Visser, "Dashcam video appears
to show Fort Worth cop shooting man in the back." *CNN*
(December 30, 2016). https://www.cnn.com/2016/12/30/us/
fort-worth-texas-police-shooting/index.html

9. Jack Fink, "Now Paralyzed, Fort Worth Man Shot By Police
Speaks Out For First Time." *CBS DFW* (February 17, 2017).
https://dfw.cbslocal.com/2017/02/14/now-paralyzed-fort-
worth-man-shot-by-police-speaks-out-for-first-time/.

10. Josh Levin, "The Judge Who Coined 'Indict a Ham Sandwich' Was Himself Indicted." *Slate* (November 25, 2014). https://slate.com/human-interest/2014/11/sol-wachtler-the-judge-who-coined-indict-a-ham-sandwich-was-himself-indicted.html.

TASED, HOGTIED, AND...

Khari Illidge didn't know where he was. The twenty-five-year-old Black man was experiencing a mental health crisis as he wandered through the suburbs of Columbus, Georgia, one night in 2013. He was visibly unstable, naked, and covered in scratches.

An onlooker had spotted him and called the police to report a trespasser. When the officers arrived on the scene, they found Khari wandering along a quiet road and asked him to stop.

Khari didn't comply, so the cops tased him until he collapsed to the ground. But they didn't stop.

As the young man lay face down, convulsing on the concrete, one of the officers tased him thirteen more times. Other officers attempted to secure Khari's wrists and ankles together in a restraint known as the hogtie—a technique that most police departments had long outlawed. A 385-pound officer knelt on Khari's upper back, crushing his lungs until he expelled froth and blood from his mouth in a red foam.

"They treated him like an animal," said Gladis Callwood, Khari's mother.

Khari was pronounced dead on arrival when he finally got to the hospital. The cause of death was listed as "cardiac arrest."

Gladis filed a lawsuit against the officers involved in the incident. But Judge W. Harold Albritton, presiding over a federal district court in Montgomery, Alabama, granted the officers qualified immunity. *He ruled that there was no precedent on the books establishing that tasing a man nineteen times before crushing him slowly to death in the street was unlawful.*

"Officers responded to an unarmed Black man in mental health crisis by using extreme force that had no purpose other than to inflict pain," Sherrilyn Ifill, President and Director-Counsel at the NAACP Legal Defense and Educational Fund (NAACP-LDF), said when discussing the case. "Using force in this way serves no legitimate law enforcement purpose and clearly violates the Fourth Amendment's protection against unreasonable seizures."

The NAACP-LDF took the case all the way to the Supreme Court on behalf of Gladis Callwood. But the Court rejected the appeal.

***

References

1. https://www.reuters.com/investigates/special-report/
   usa-police-immunity-scotus/
2. https://www.naacpldf.org/files/our-work/Callwood%20
   Cert%20Petition%20FINAL.pdf
3. https://woldcnews.com/162
4. https://caselaw.findlaw.com/us-11th-circuit/1889970.html

THE ONLY WAY TO FIX QUALIFIED IMMUNITY IS TO END IT

Elizabeth B. Wydra and David H. Gans,
Constitutional Accountability Center

The Fourteenth Amendment was drafted more than 150 years ago, in part, to prevent—and redress—the same police violence against African Americans our nation suffers to this very day. That Amendment, added to the Constitution against a backdrop of horrific massacres in which white police officers killed hundreds of African Americans in cold blood, provides Congress with broad power to curb unjustified use of force by police—and gives the people the right to demand the equal justice the Amendment promises.

The Fourteenth Amendment was the nation's response to abuses in the South in the wake of the end of slavery. In the aftermath of the Civil War, the South sought to reimpose the racist oppression of slavery, though the institution itself had been formally abolished by the Thirteenth Amendment. Racialized police abuse lies at the core of what the Fourteenth Amendment sought to prohibit.[1] Police made mass arrests to keep African Americans in subordinate status and prevent them from enjoying meaningful freedom. Police broke into the homes of African Americans and sought to steal their personal property. Police beat and killed African American people, while turning a blind eye to the crimes committed against them.

In response to these abuses, the Fourteenth Amendment promised true freedom and equality. It sought to vindicate the simple and fundamental demands of African Americans newly freed from bondage that "now we are free we do not want to be hunted," we want to be "treated like human beings."[2] The Fourteenth Amendment wrote into our national charter the idea that Black lives matter, seeking to put an end to indiscriminate state-sanctioned violence against African Americans. It promised bodily integrity and human dignity to all, regardless of the color of their skin.

In 1871, three years after the ratification of the Fourteenth Amendment, the Reconstruction Congress passed legislation—Section 1983—to enforce the

Fourteenth Amendment and ensure that individuals could go to federal court to redress constitutional violations and obtain justice. Against the backdrop of horrific state and mob violence, Section 1983 gave those victimized by the abuse of power a critical tool to hold government officials accountable in a court of law.

The accountability contained within Section 1983, however, remains elusive, because the remedy Congress designed has been gutted by the Supreme Court's invention of qualified immunity. Through the creation and aggressive expansion of this judge-made doctrine, the Supreme Court has effectively closed the courthouse doors for many whose constitutional rights have been violated, and allowed rights to be trampled and lives to be taken with impunity.

The qualified immunity doctrine enables officials to have such suits against them dismissed as long as their conduct did not violate "clearly established" constitutional rights.[3] In practice, this has come to mean that injured plaintiffs cannot proceed with their suits unless they can point to a prior decision establishing that precisely the same conduct violates the law.[4] Worse still, when a court determines that the illegality of an official's conduct is not "clearly established," the court can dismiss the suit without determining whether that conduct actually violated the law.[5] This means that the next time an official harms someone through the same conduct, there will still be no clearly established law for the victim to rely on—and it will still be impossible to hold anyone liable for violating the Constitution. As a result, the law remains frozen in place and justice is denied to victims of government abuse of power.

Qualified immunity is particularly pernicious in the context of policing. It erodes the enforcement of constitutional rights, undermines the rule of law, and denies justice to those victimized by the police, letting the cycle of racialized policing and police brutality repeat over and over again. The long line of police killings of unarmed Black people—George Floyd and Breonna Taylor among the most recent—is the result of a system that breeds police unaccountability. We cannot redress the scourge of centuries of white supremacist, state-sanctioned brutality if police may violate constitutional rights with impunity.

But qualified immunity shields more than police misconduct from accountability. Qualified immunity applies to a wide array of public officials, such as prison guards, school administrators, and social workers, and governs a wide range of unconstitutional government action, including deprivation of freedom of speech, infliction of cruel and unusual punishment, and denial of due process. In all these settings, qualified immunity prevents government officials from being held accountable for violating constitutionally protected rights.

Congress must redeem the promise of the Fourteenth Amendment by ending qualified immunity once and for all. Congress should not tolerate qualified immunity in any area of the law. If the judiciary is unwilling to fix its own mistake, Congress must step in to make clear that government officials should be held accountable when they violate people's constitutional rights.

Ending qualified immunity would make the promise of the Fourteenth Amendment more real, enhance government accountability, encourage courts to play their historic role of redressing abuse of power, punish wrongdoing by those sworn to uphold the law, and create an incentive for governments to properly train their officers to respect constitutional rights. It would be a long overdue step in the direction of meaningful justice, down a path marked by the Fourteenth Amendment.

Our Constitution's system of accountability demands that those victimized by abuse of power can go to court to seek redress. We cannot rein in abuse of power if courts give state officials a free pass when they violate our fundamental rights. Qualified immunity must be eliminated.

Elizabeth B. Wydra is the President of the Constitutional Accountability Center. David H. Gans is the Director of the

Human Rights, Civil Rights, and Citizenship Program at the Constitutional Accountability Center.

References

1. David H. Gans, *"We Do Not Want to Be Hunted": The Right to Be Secure and Our Constitutional Story of Race and Policing*, 11 Colum. J. Race & L. (forthcoming 2021), https://papers.ssrn.com/sol3/papers.cfm?abstract_id=3622599.
2. Letter from Mississippi Freedpeople to the Governor of Mississippi (Dec. 3, 1865), reprinted in Freedom: *A Documentary History of Emancipation, 1861-1867, Ser. 3: Vol. 1: Land and Labor, 1865*, at 857 (Steven Hahn et al. eds. 2017).
3. *Harlow v. Fitzgerald*, 457 U.S. 800, 818 (1982); *Mullenix v. Luna*, 136 S. Ct. 305, 308 (2015); *District of Columbia v. Wesby*, 138 S. Ct. 577, 589-90 (2018).
4. *Ashcroft v. Al-Kidd*, 563 U.S. 731, 741 (2011) (stating that qualified immunity permits liability only when "existing precedent" is so clear that the "constitutional question [is] beyond debate").
5. *Pearson v. Callahan*, 555 U.S. 223 (2009).

UNDERCOVER AND ABOVE THE LAW

James King, a white twenty-one-year-old Grand Valley State University student, had just left his internship for the day and was walking to his second job. "I was calling my sister at the time," James said, "and somewhat distracted by looking at my phone."

Suddenly, James was approached by two men who took him aside and demanded to know who he was. When James told them his name, they threw him up against a car and took James' wallet from his back pocket.

James' heart raced. *I'm being mugged,* he thought. He broke away and started to run.

"Call the police!" James screamed.

Then James hit the concrete. The men tackled him and began to beat him and pound his head into the ground.

"They're beating him up, like, they're literally assaulting him," a bystander told 911.

Then the men got James in a chokehold and he blacked out.

What James had thought were "muggers" were actually plainclothes officers looking for a petty-theft suspect—James didn't even fit the description of the person they were looking for. They mistook James for someone else, and nearly beat him to death.

When uniformed officers arrived in response to the 911 call, they covered their tracks by closing ranks. They pressured witnesses to delete photo and video evidence "for officer safety." And they charged James with three violent felonies.

James was taken to the hospital and handcuffed to his bed like a criminal. Later he was transferred to a jail cell. He had a mugshot taken. He spent the night in a cell, his face swollen with bruises. His family had to post $50,000 bail to get him out.

For the three violent felonies, James was offered a plea bargain, but he refused. James stood by his principles. He had done nothing wrong.

"Instead of admitting they were wrong, they charged me with three felonies," James said.

Because of his decision, James had to stand trial. If found guilty, he could have been sentenced to up to ten years in prison—for a crime he didn't commit.

It took six months and cost his parents their entire life savings to pay for legal fees, but the jury unanimously acquitted James of all charges.

Although it was a huge relief, James found that it didn't ease the burden of the trauma and humiliation he had endured.

"After the assault, I dropped out of Grand Valley State University," James said. "It's not just the incident as it happened, when it happened, but all the repercussions since then—missed job opportunities . . . I cannot work federal jobs."

After his court case, James sued the police officers.

"These officers did something that was illegal and then charged me for crimes, and the system closed around them and helped them get away with that," he said. "There is zero accountability."

But the court granted qualified immunity to the officers.

The Institute of Justice (IJ), a libertarian nonprofit that represents individuals who are denied their constitutional rights, took an interest in James' case. IJ attorney Patrick Jaicomo filed a federal lawsuit on behalf of James against the officers, and is bringing it to the Supreme Court.

"For the United States Supreme Court to make things right in James' case . . . it needs to revisit this concept of qualified immunity," Jaicomo said.

***

References

1. https://ij.org/case/brownback-v-king/
2. https://www.youtube.com/watch?v=k065AamnXxg
3. https://www.scotusblog.com/case-files/cases/
   brownback-v-king/

DRIVING WHILE BLACK

In July 2013, Clarence Jamison, a Black man, was cruising down the interstate in a new Mercedes convertible. He was driving back home to South Carolina from a vacation in Phoenix.

As he drove through Pelahatchie, Mississippi, Clarence passed a police cruiser parked on the right shoulder. The officer spotted him driving by, and turned on his cruiser lights to pull him over. Clarence brought his car to a stop by the side of the road.

"License and registration?" The officer asked.

Clarence handed him his driver's license, car insurance, and the paperwork on the vehicle. Since the car was newly purchased, it sported a temporary tag instead of a standard license plate. The officer would later claim that he stopped Clarence because the car's temporary tag was "folded over to where [he] couldn't see it."

The officer returned to his patrol car to verify Clarence's information and conduct a background check. The check came back moments later: Clarence was clear.

The officer decided to run another check. This time he contacted the National Criminal Information Center (NCIC) and asked the dispatcher to run a deeper criminal history check on Clarence, as well as the VIN number on the car. The result would take a little time.

The officer returned to the Mercedes and handed the documents back to Clarence. Thinking he was free to go, Clarence prepared to leave.

Then the officer asked if he could search the car.

"For what?" asked Clarence.

"For anything illegal," the officer replied.

Clarence refused. The officer asked him again—this time lying about a report he had received that the car had ten kilograms of cocaine in it. Again, Clarence refused the search. He knew it was well within his Constitutional rights to deny a search without a valid reason or a warrant. But the officer wouldn't let it go.

The officer asked two more times to search Clarence's car, each time moving his hand further into the vehicle, and at one point patting the inside of the passenger's side door.

After repeatedly refusing, Clarence gave in and let the officer examine the vehicle.

The officer searched "from the engine compartment to the trunk to the undercarriage to underneath the engine to the back seats to anywhere to account for all the voids inside the vehicle."

He didn't find anything.

By this time, the results of the secondary NCIC search came back. Clarence's license was clear.

Then the officer requested a canine search. Again, Clarence refused. The officer persisted and Clarence eventually agreed.

The dog found nothing illegal in the vehicle.

Nearly two hours after he was first stopped, Clarence Jamison left the traffic stop with substantial damage to his car. It seemed apparent that he had been pulled over simply for being a Black man driving a nice car. Although Clarence got away from the incident unharmed, he knew things could have easily turned out very differently.

"When I first got home, I couldn't sleep. So I was up for, like—I didn't even sleep when I got home. I think I got some rest the next day because I was still mad just thinking about it and then when all this killing and stuff come[s] on TV, that's, like, a flashback. I said, man, this could have went this way. It had me thinking all kind[s] of stuff because it was not even called for," Clarence recalled.

Clarence sued the officer and the City of Pelahatchie for multiple violations of his Fourteenth Amendment rights. He cited the psychological harm he suffered as a result of the stop, as well as the physical damage to his car—nearly $4,000.

The court ruled that the officer's decision to pull Clarence over was protected by qualified immunity. So was his search of the vehicle—despite the fact that Clarence's rights had clearly been violated in the process.

But in his opinion, District Court Judge Carlton Reeves wrote the following:

"Under that law, the officer who transformed a short traffic stop into an almost two-hour, life-altering ordeal is entitled to qualified immunity. The officer's motion seeking as much is therefore granted. But let us not be fooled by legal jargon. Immunity is not exoneration. And the harm in this case to one man sheds light on the harm done to the nation by this manufactured doctrine."

***

References

1. https://graphics.thomsonreuters.com/srepfiles/2020/qi-four-master/en/pdf/3-16CV00595_Reeves_08-04-2020.pdf

2. https://www.newsweek.com/federal-judge-slams-supreme-court-while-granting-cop-qualified-immunity-1522847#:~:text=Jamison%20filed%20a%20lawsuit%20against,for%20damages%20and%20psychological%20suffering.

3. https://www.npr.org/2020/08/06/899489809/judge-shielding-cop-via-qualified-immunity-asks-whether-it-belongs-in-dustbin

JUSTICE REEVES–BUMPER

The following is a short excerpt from an Order Granting Qualified Immunity File dated August 4, 2020, by Justice Carlton Reeves of the U.S. District Court for the Southern District of Mississippi.

ABOVE THE LAW

No. 3:16-CV-595-CWR-LRA

CLARENCE JAMISON,

Plaintiff,

v.

NICK MCCLENDON,
In his individual capacity,

Defendant.

ORDER GRANTING QUALIFIED IMMUNITY

Before CARLTON W. REEVES, *District Judge.*

Clarence Jamison wasn't jaywalking.[1]

He wasn't outside playing with a toy gun.[2]

---

[1] That was Michael Brown. *See* Max Ehrenfreund, *The risks of walking while black in Ferguson,* WASH. POST (Mar. 4, 2015).

[2] That was 12-year-old Tamir Rice. *See* Zola Ray, *This Is The Toy Gun That Got Tamir Rice Killed 3 Years Ago Today,* NEWSWEEK (Nov. 22, 2017).

He didn't look like a "suspicious person."[3]

He wasn't suspected of "selling loose, untaxed cigarettes."[4]

He wasn't suspected of passing a counterfeit $20 bill.[5]

He didn't look like anyone suspected of a crime.[6]

He wasn't mentally ill and in need of help.[7]

He wasn't assisting an autistic patient who had wandered away from a group home.[8]

---

[3] That was Elijah McClain. *See* Claire Lampen, *What We Know About the Killing of Elijah McClain*, THE CUT (July 5, 2020).

[4] That was Eric Garner. *See* Assoc. Press, *From Eric Garner's death to firing of NYPD officer: A timeline of key events*, USA TODAY (Aug. 20, 2019).

[5] That was George Floyd. *See* Jemima McEvoy, *New Transcripts Reveal How Suspicion Over Counterfeit Money Escalated Into The Death Of George Floyd*, FORBES (July 8, 2020).

[6] That was Philando Castile and Tony McDade. *See* Andy Mannix, *Police audio: Officer stopped Philando Castile on robbery suspicion*, STAR TRIB. (July 12, 2016); Meredith Deliso, *LGBTQ community calls for justice after Tony McDade, a black trans man, shot and killed by police*, ABC NEWS (June 2, 2020).

[7] That was Jason Harrison. *See* Byron Pitts et al., *The Deadly Consequences When Police Lack Proper Training to Handle Mental Illness Calls*, ABC NEWS (Sept. 30, 2015).

[8] That was Charles Kinsey. *See Florida policeman shoots autistic man's unarmed black therapist*, BBC (July 21, 2016).

He wasn't walking home from an after-school job.[9]

He wasn't walking back from a restaurant.[10]

He wasn't hanging out on a college campus.[11]

He wasn't standing outside of his apartment.[12]

He wasn't inside his apartment eating ice cream.[13]

He wasn't sleeping in his bed.[14]

He wasn't sleeping in his car.[15]

---

[9] That was 17-year-old James Earl Green. *See* Robert Luckett, *In 50 Years from Gibbs-Green Deaths to Ahmaud Arbery Killing, White Supremacy Still Lives,* JACKSON FREE PRESS (May 8, 2020); *see also* Robert Luckett, *50 Years Ago, Police Fired on Students at a Historically Black College,* N.Y. TIMES (May 14, 2020); Rachel James-Terry & L.A. Warren, *'All hell broke loose': Memories still vivid of Jackson State shooting 50 years ago,* CLARION LEDGER (May 15, 2020).

[10] That was Ben Brown. *See* Notice to Close File, U.S. DEP'T OF JUSTICE, CIVIL RIGHTS DIV. (Mar. 24, 2017), *available at* https://www.justice.gov/crt/case-document/benjamin-brown-notice-close-file; *see also* Jackson State Univ., Center for University-Based Development, *The Life of Benjamin Brown, 50 Years Later,* W. JACKSON (May 11, 2017).

[11] That was Phillip Gibbs. *See* James-Terry & Warren, *supra.*

[12] That was Amadou Diallo. *See Police fired 41 shots when they killed Amadou Diallo. His mom hopes today's protests will bring change.,* CBS NEWS (June 9, 2020).

[13] That was Botham Jean. *See* Bill Hutchinson, *Death of an innocent man: Timeline of wrong-apartment murder trial of Amber Guyger,* ABC NEWS (Oct. 2, 2019).

[14] That was Breonna Taylor. *See* Amina Elahi, *'Sleeping While Black': Louisville Police Kill Unarmed Black Woman,* NPR (May 13, 2020).

[15] That was Rayshard Brooks. *See* Jacob Sullum, *Was the Shooting of Rayshard Brooks 'Lawful but Awful'?,* REASON (June 15, 2020).

He didn't make an "improper lane change."[16]

He didn't have a broken tail light.[17]

He wasn't driving over the speed limit.[18]

He wasn't driving under the speed limit.[19]

No, Clarence Jamison was a Black man driving a Mercedes convertible.

As he made his way home to South Carolina from a vacation in Arizona, Jamison was pulled over and subjected to one hundred and ten minutes of an armed police officer badgering him, pressuring him, lying to him, and then searching his car top-to-bottom for drugs.

Nothing was found. Jamison isn't a drug courier. He's a welder.

Unsatisfied, the officer then brought out a canine to sniff the car. The dog found nothing. So nearly two hours after it started, the officer left Jamison by the side of the road to put his car back together.

---

[16] That was Sandra Bland. *See* Ben Mathis-Lilley & Elliott Hannon, *A Black Woman Named Sandra Bland Got Pulled Over in Texas and Died in Jail Three Days Later. Why?*, SLATE (July 16, 2015).

[17] That was Walter Scott. *See* Michael E. Miller et al., *How a cellphone video led to murder charges against a cop in North Charleston, S.C.*, WASH. POST (Apr. 8, 2015).

[18] That was Hannah Fizer. *See* Luke Nozicka, *'Where's the gun?': Family of Sedalia woman killed by deputy skeptical of narrative*, KANSAS CITY STAR (June 15, 2020).

[19] That was Ace Perry. *See* Jodi Leese Glusco, *Run-in with Sampson deputy leaves driver feeling unsafe*, WRAL (Feb. 14, 2020).

Thankfully, Jamison left the stop with his life. Too many others have not.[20]

The Constitution says everyone is entitled to equal protection of the law – even at the hands of law enforcement. Over the decades, however, judges have invented a legal doctrine to protect law enforcement officers from having to face any consequences for wrongdoing. The doctrine is called "qualified immunity." In real life it operates like absolute immunity.

In a recent qualified immunity case, the Fourth Circuit wrote:

> Although we recognize that our police officers are often asked to make split-second decisions, we expect them to do so with respect for the dignity and worth of black lives.[21]

This Court agrees. Tragically, thousands have died at the hands of law enforcement over the years, and the death toll continues to rise.[22] Countless more have suffered from other

---

[20] *See, e.g.*, Mike Baker et al., *Three Words. 70 cases. The tragic History of 'I Can't Breathe.'*, N.Y. TIMES (June 29, 2020) (discussing the deaths of Eric Garner, George Floyd, and 68 other people killed while in law enforcement custody whose last words included the statement, "I can't breathe.").

[21] *Estate of Jones v. City of Martinsburg, W. Virginia*, 961 F.3d 661, 673 (4th Cir. 2020), *as amended* (June 10, 2020).

[22] Mark Berman et al., *Protests spread over police shootings. Police promised reforms. Every year, they still shoot and kill nearly 1,000 people.*, WASH. POST (June 8, 2020) ("Since 2015, police have shot and killed 5,400 people."); *see also* Alicia Victoria Lozano, *Fatal Encounters: One man is tracking every officer-involved killing in the U.S.*, NBC NEWS (July 11, 2020), ("As of July 10, Fatal Encounters lists more than 28,400 deaths dating to Jan. 1, 2000. The entries include both headline-making cases and thousands of lesser-known deaths.").

forms of abuse and misconduct by police.[23] Qualified immunity has served as a shield for these officers, protecting them from accountability.

This Court is required to apply the law as stated by the Supreme Court. Under that law, the officer who transformed a short traffic stop into an almost two-hour, life-altering ordeal is entitled to qualified immunity. The officer's motion seeking as much is therefore granted.

But let us not be fooled by legal jargon. Immunity is not exoneration. And the harm in this case to one man sheds light on the harm done to the nation by this manufactured doctrine.

As the Fourth Circuit concluded, "This has to stop."[24]

CALL THE REAL COPS

Kendole Joseph, a Black twenty-seven-year-old father of two, was in the middle of a schizophrenic episode. Nervous and shaking, he was weaving his way down the street when police approached him.

He walked faster, pulling on the door handles of locked cars, looking for a place to hide. Then he darted into a convenience store.

"Help me, help me, somebody call the cops!" he pleaded to the manager. "They're trying to kill me!"

Ten police officers burst into the store. "Freeze!" the cops yelled.

Kendole jumped behind the counter and curled up into a ball on the ground.

"Help me!" He pleaded. "Call the real cops."

"My name is Kendole Joseph!" he yelled. "I don't have a weapon! Please call my mother!"

A 300-pound officer jumped behind the counter and pinned Kendole to the ground, while other officers jolted Kendole with their tasers and kicked him repeatedly.

Kendole never fought back. He remained curled up in the fetal position, his hands covering his face, flailing as officers struck him.

The ordeal lasted eight minutes.

By the time the police dragged Kendole, bloody and beaten, in shackles to the patrol car he was unresponsive. Kendole was rushed to the hospital and pronounced dead two days later. He had suffered twenty-six blunt-force injuries to his face, chest, back, scrotum, testes, and other areas.

In the aftermath of Kendole's death, his family worked with civil rights activists and attorneys to sue the cops. "My brother was innocent," his sister told the press. "he was beaten and tased" to death.

In a rare partial victory, the courts rejected qualified immunity for two of the ten officers for their failure to de-escalate and for their excessive use of force. But the other eight officers who witnessed and participated in the violence were all granted qualified immunity.

***

References

1. https://www.courthousenews.com/wp-content/uploads/2020/11/proportionalresponse.pdf
2. https://reason.com/2020/11/25/cops-who-beat-and-killed-an-innocent-man-are-not-entitled-to-qualified-immunity/

3. https://www.nola.com/news/crime_police/article_964fa3de-c100-579b-b3b9-d208ed18f1aa.html#:~:text=Kendole%20Joseph%2C%2027%2C%20died%20in,restrained%20him%20using%20a%20Taser.&text=Officers%20said%20they%20used%20a,He%20died%20Feb.
4. https://www.dailykos.com/stories/2020/12/3/1999745/-Fifth-Circuit-denies-police-immunity-in-deadly-beating-of-unarmed-Louisiana-man
5. https://www.wwltv.com/article/news/local/jefferson/family-wants-officers-fired-re-training-after-kendole-joseph-death/289-443353986

HIDE THE TEA

Robert and Adlynn Harte are both white, retired CIA analysts with top-level security clearances. After a career spent serving their country, the couple settled in quiet Leawood, Kansas, with their two young children.

In 2011, Missouri highway patrol officer Jim Wingo was running "Operation Constant Gardener." He sat in the parking lot of a gardening store in Kansas City, writing down the license plate numbers of all the customers. He spotted Robert and his two children leaving the store carrying a small bag. Robert was there purchasing supplies for his thirteen-year-old son's school project, growing tomatoes.

Eight months later, the officer shared his database of license plates with local law enforcement agencies, triggering an investigation into the Harte family.

Cops collected and searched the Hartes' trash three times. When a deputy came across leftover loose-leaf tea, he tossed it aside. But the second time, the cops got suspicious. They drafted up a search warrant application, claiming that each time they searched the trash they found between a quarter of a cup and a cup of "saturated marijuana plant material." They pointed to Robert's trip to the gardening store as evidence of an "indoor marijuana growing operation."

They got an assistant district attorney and judge to approve the warrant application. Then they launched their early-morning raid on April 20, 2012.

It was 7:30 a.m. when the cops pounded on the Hartes' front door. There was "screaming and loud banging, so hard that the walls were rattling." Robert opened the door, and seven deputies and a pack of drug-sniffing K-9s flooded into his home. The deputies were wearing bullet-proof vests and carrying their AR-15s and Glocks at the "low-ready position."

"On the ground," the deputies ordered. Robert, Adlynn, and the children lay on their stomachs at gun-point while the cops raided their home.

The raid lasted for hours. A concerned neighbor stopped by and offered to take the children, but the cops refused. In the end, they found nothing.

The cops were furious that they got nothing from the raid. "You're lying to me," a sergeant said when he heard the news. "SON OF A BITCH!!!" A lieutenant screamed. "Nothing???"

A lab technician later definitively stated that the tea leaves didn't "look anything like marijuana leaves," either to the naked eye or under a microscope.

Still, that night, the cops held a press conference to promote their "successful" drug raids.

They announced that they caught "average Johnson County families," including those "in good neighborhoods" like Leawood, where the Hartes lived and where their neighbors witnessed the raid. In reality, they seized zero marijuana plants that day. The cops did not exonerate the Harte family, leaving their neighbors with the impression that they were criminals.

So the Harte family hired a lawyer and sued the cops.

It wasn't enough. A federal judge would not even let their case go before a jury because he thought that "no reasonable jury" could conclude that the cops had violated the Hartes' constitutional rights. Even if the cops broke the law, the judge ruled, they were entitled to qualified immunity.

Most people can't afford expensive appeals, so that's where it normally would have ended. In this case, the libertarian Cato Institute offered to help the Hartes appeal, pro bono. An appeals court was much more critical of the cops, with one judge writing:

The defendants in this case caused an unjustified governmental intrusion into the Hartes' home based on nothing more than junk science, an incompetent investigation, and a publicity stunt. The Fourth Amendment does not condone this conduct, and neither can I.

The lawsuit dragged through the courts for years, the cops were denied full qualified immunity, and the Hartes eventually agreed to settle the case against the police for $150,000.

***

References

1. https://www.kansascity.com/news/local/article187836344.html
2. https://www.washingtonpost.com/news/the-watch/wp/2015/12/28/federal-judge-drinking-tea-shopping-at-a-gardening-store-is-probable-cause-for-a-swat-raid-on-your-home/.
3. https://www.cato.org/publications/legal-briefs/harte-v-board-commissioners-johnson-county-kansas.
4. https://law.justia.com/cases/federal/appellate-courts/ca10/18-3091/18-3091-2019-10-04.html
5. https://www.hollandhart.com/the-law-of-the-case-doctrine-and-mandate-rule

6. https://ecf.ksd.uscourts.gov/cgi-bin/show_public_doc?2013cv2586-340

7. https://reason.com/2019/10/30/victims-of-marijuana-raid-based-on-tea-in-the-trash-get-another-chance-to-hold-cops-responsible/

8. https://www.ca10.uscourts.gov/opinions/16/16-3014.pdf

9. https://www.usnews.com/news/best-states/kansas/articles/2020-04-18/kansas-couple-targeted-in-bungled-pot-raid-settles-lawsuit

10. https://apnews.com/article/231b414d04aa36ldfb8e82e21bef8c39

11. https://www.kcur.org/news/2020-05-04/leawood-family-that-was-the-target-of-a-botched-swat-raid-settles-lawsuit-for-150-000

TAKE IT FROM ME, A FORMER COP: QUALIFIED IMMUNITY MUST END

After graduating college, I worked to reelect Tom Bradley, the first African-American mayor in Los Angeles. He'd spent his career in the Los Angeles Police Department, rising to Lieutenant—the highest rank then awarded in the department to a Black man. I didn't know much about urban policy, and he suggested I learn more by entering the reserve program of the LAPD.

I joined the department in 1981, graduated from the police academy at the top of my class, and was offered my choice of assignments. I chose routine patrol in Watts, the largely African-American inner city that revolted in riots sixteen years earlier and was still the city's poorest and most violent precinct. If I was going to serve and learn, that was the place.

Working nine years of weekends in uniform from a black-and-white patrol car, I answered thousands of 911 radio calls—mostly from low-income women of color being abused by men. That was a violent period in the city's history, with 1,000 murders in a single year. I averaged about one felony arrest each shift I worked, drawing my gun every night I worked while subduing violent suspects. The sole shootout I experienced started with the suspect firing first. Police work is indeed dangerous.

And yet, society has the right to expect professional restraint from its law enforcers. The LAPD's training was rigorous: I spent 540 hours at the academy and had extensive field training thereafter. We were well-equipped, with body armor and lots of resources to rely on when needed. Two officers were assigned to each patrol car in my district, to reinforce our safety and appropriately handle citizens' calls for help.

Law enforcement officials who destroy the public's trust by enacting their own, unwarranted violence on innocent citizens need to be held accountable. Giving them a pass under qualified immunity prevents justice for those officers, and signals to others who wear a badge that they, too, can wreak havoc without consequence. We have a criminal justice system to punish the offender and discourage others from committing crimes. Exempting the very people entrusted with enforcing the law is dangerous policy, leads to gross injustice, and shows the community that law enforcement officers are above the law.

This immunity must end.

Duane Peterson has dedicated his four- decade career toward justice—with stops along the way in law enforcement, political organizing, government service in the executive and legislative branches, and values-led business.

SURRENDERING WHILE BLACK

Alexander Baxter, a homeless, middle-aged Black man, knew he was caught. He sat frozen, his hands in the air, watching a K-9 circle the basement of a house in Nashville, Tennessee.

Alexander had broken into the house fleeing from another house burglary with the police in pursuit.

"Show me your hands!" an officer yelled, shining a flashlight and pointing his gun at Alexander. The K-9 paced back and forth, barking.

One of the officers grabbed the dog by its collar. It kept barking and rearing up at Alexander.

Alexander held his hands higher in the air. He surrendered.

Then, without warning, the officer sicced the dog on him.

The K-9 attacked, sinking its teeth into Alexander's armpit. The bites were so bad that Alexander had to be rushed to the hospital.

Since the Metropolitan Nashville Police Department denied Alexander's internal complaints and appeals, he filed a handwritten civil rights complaint in federal court from jail. That's when the American Civil Liberties Union (ACLU) got involved.

In cases of police brutality, the Supreme Court requires lower court judges to ignore **whether any laws were broken and dismiss the case, unless another police officer *in the same jurisdiction* had been found guilty previously in a similar situation.**

The lawyer knew that the court had already ruled that it was illegal to release a K-9 on a suspect who had surrendered, and that gave Alexander a good shot at justice.

But at trial, the judge ruled that since in the previous case the suspect had surrendered by lying down, and Alexander had surrendered by *sitting on the ground with his hands up,* that the cases **were not similar enough.** So the judge invoked qualified immunity and let the cops off scot-free.

The ACLU tried to appeal the case to the Supreme Court, but they upheld the lower court's decision.

Supreme Court Justice Clarence Thomas objected to the decision, writing that he had long had "doubts about our qualified immunity jurisprudence."

***

References

1. *Baxter v. Harris et al* complaint
2. *Baxter v. Harris et al* amicus brief (Cato Institute)
3. *Baxter v. Harris et al* brief in opposition
4. *Baxter v. Harris et al* reply in support of petition
5. *Baxter v. Harris et al* petition for cert
6. *POLITICO* article by Josh Gerstein (6/5/20)
7. *Reason.com* article by C.J. Ciaramella (4/8/19)
8. Reuters article by Lawrence Hurley and Andrew Chung (5/8/20)
9. *Zadeh v. Robinson* (dissent of Judge Willett)
10. SCOTUS *Baxter v. Bracey* et al (dissent of J. Thomas)
11. ACLU, *Baxter v. Bracey* page

SCHOOL DROP-OFF

Malaika Brooks, a thirty-three-year-old Black woman, was driving her eleven-year-old son to school one morning when she hit a speed trap. The speed limit dropped from thirty-five to twenty miles per hour, and the police alleged she was going 12 miles over the limit.

The cops pulled Malaika over, checked her license and registration, and then wrote her a speeding ticket.

"Sign the ticket," the officer commanded, handing her the ticket.

"I'll take the ticket, but I won't sign it," Malaika said. Signing the ticket would be an acknowledgment of guilt, she thought. This wasn't the case, but the signature was required by law.

That's when the officer called for backup. More cops came on the scene and demanded that Malaika sign the citation. When a supervisor finally arrived, rather than de-escalating the situation, he told the other cops to "book her."

"Get out of the car!" the officer yelled, removing Malaika's keys from the ignition. "Do you know what this is?" he asked, threatening her with a taser. "Do you know what this is?"

"I am pregnant," Malaika said, "I'm less than sixty days from having my baby." Malaika was seven months pregnant. Her son was in the back seat, watching.

The cops huddled.

"Well, where do you want to do it?" one officer asked.

"Well, don't do it in her stomach," another said. "Do it in her thigh."

In less than a minute, the cops tased Malaika three times, sending 50,000 volts into her thigh, arm, and neck.

They gave her no time between tasings to reconsider her actions or agree to get out of the car.

When she slumped over, the cops dragged her out of the car, crying, and laid her facedown on the street. Then they handcuffed her and placed her under arrest.

Malaika was rushed to the hospital. Doctors feared her rapid heartbeat could be a problem for her unborn child. Fortunately, her baby was born healthy.

"This is outrageous—that something like this could happen to a pregnant woman, in front of an elementary school, at 8:30 in the morning, to someone who posed no threat whatsoever," Malaika's lawyer said.

Malaika took the cops to court. The judge pointed out that Malaika wasn't trying to flee, posed no danger to anyone, and the situation was not urgent enough to justify the cops' brutal actions. The judge decided that a jury should hear the case, and denied the cops qualified immunity.

The cops appealed the decision, again claiming qualified immunity. The appeals court overruled the lower court and defended the cops' actions. In her dissent, one of the judges stated that Malaika's refusal to sign the traffic ticket wasn't even "an arrestable offense." The judge was shocked at her colleagues' conclusions, writing:

> I fail utterly to comprehend how my colleagues are able to conclude that it was objectively reasonable to use any force against Brooks, let alone three activations of a taser, in response to such a trivial offense.

***

References

1. https://www.nytimes.com/2012/05/15/us/police-taser-use-on-pregnant-woman-goes-before-supreme-court.html
2. http://cdn.ca9.uscourts.gov/datastore/opinions/2011/10/17/08-15567.pdf
3. https://www.cnn.com/2012/05/29/justice/scotus-taser-shocks/index.html
4. http://www.aele.org/law/2011all12/2011-12MLJ101.pdf

5. https://www.theskanner.com/news/northwest/21826-seattle-settles-out-of-court-in-malaika-brooks-case

6. https://emancipatenc.org/why-qualified-immunity-for-cops-must-be-stopped-the-story-of-malaika-brooks/

7. http://sblog.s3.amazonaws.com/wp-content/uploads/2012/03/11-898-Seattle-Cert-Amicus.pdf

8. https://www.seattlepi.com/local/article/Pregnant-woman-Tasered-by-police-is-convicted-1172950.php

THE REASONING BEHIND QUALIFIED IMMUNITY

The theory underlying qualified immunity is that a police officer (an officer of the law) is not expected to know that something they might do is unlawful *unless* another cop has previously been convicted for breaking that particular law in their jurisdiction.

So, if a case of police brutality or worse is brought to a judge, the judge is **legally required to ignore that a crime has been committed** if there has not been a previous conviction of a police officer for exactly the same crime in that jurisdiction.

This means that police (law enforcement officers) are not expected to know the Bill of Rights, unless a police officer in their jurisdiction has previously been convicted of violating a particular right.

But it gets worse. Even if there has been a previous conviction of a police officer for violating the same law, if the violation did not occur in *exactly the same way,* the judge is required to throw the case out. Here's a real-life example:

A police officer was convicted of siccing his attack dog on a man who had surrendered by lying on the ground. A few years later, another officer sicced his attack dog on a man who surrendered by sitting on the ground with his hands in the air. That case was thrown out by the judge because it was not similar enough. And the Supreme Court upheld it. (See the chapter "Surrendering While Black.")

And then there's the Catch-22: Since it's not possible to even get a trial of a police officer who is the first in their jurisdiction to break a particular law, there can never be a previous conviction and therefore police officers who break that law can never be brought to trial.

You might say, "That doesn't make sense."

Exactly.

And that's why qualified immunity must be overturned.

UNARMED AND NOT DANGEROUS

On July 10, 2014, Amy Corbitt's ten-year-old son was play-ing outside his mobile home in Coffee County, Georgia, enjoying a carefree summer day with five other neighbor-hood kids.

Suddenly, police officers stormed the scene, chasing after a robbery suspect who ran into Corbitt's front yard. Chaos ensued.

"Get down on the ground!" an officer yelled.

Everyone hit the ground, including Amy's son and the other children, two of whom were under the age of three, and all of whom were held at gunpoint, screaming and crying.

An officer handcuffed the suspect and placed a gun at his back.

Another officer aimed his gun at Bruce, the family dog, and fired twice. No one had tried to restrain the dog. No one appeared threatened by it. The police report noted that no one presented "any threat or danger to provoke."

The first shot missed. The second hit Amy's son, who was lying face down only 18 inches away, on the back of his right knee.

"I ran out the house" and saw "my little brother, on the porch, pouring blood," the boy's sister said.

The Corbitts, a white family, filed a civil rights lawsuit seeking damages to compensate for Amy's son's costly medical expenses and trauma.

The officer who shot the boy filed a motion to dismiss the case, but a federal judge allowed the lawsuit to proceed and ruled that the officer wasn't entitled to qualified immunity.

However, in 2019, a higher court reversed the ruling, granting the officer qualified immunity because no prior decision had addressed the "unique facts of this case."

Because the officer was not convicted, if another police officer acted similarly in the future, they, too, would receive qualified immunity, since no precedent was set.

In his dissent, Judge Charles Wilson defended the lower court's ruling. "Because no competent officer would fire his weapon in the direction of a nonthreatening pet while that pet was surrounded by children," Wilson wrote, "qualified immunity should not protect the officer."

***

References

1. http://graphics.thomsonreuters.com/srepfiles/qualified-immunity-intro/images/pdfs/NelsonvRivera.pdf
2. https://www.mlive.com/news/kalamazoo/2016/05/mother_of_battle_creek_teen_sh.html
3. https://wwmt.com/news/local/mother-of-teen-shot-by-officer-suing-city-of-battle-creek
4. https://www.woodtv.com/news/battle-creek-mom-suing-city-officer-who-shot-her-son/
5. https://www.youtube.com/watch?v=IXnPzifzn2E

SLEEPING WHILE BLACK

It was 7:00 a.m. and Luke Stewart, a twenty-three-year-old Black man, was fast asleep in his car on the side of the road in a residential neighborhood.

Luke was the father of two young children and got by doing landscaping and snow removal jobs in Euclid, Ohio. No one knows why he was sleeping on the side of the road, but his family suspects he was intoxicated and decided to sleep it off rather than drive home. "He wasn't perfect," his mother said, "but he was perfect enough for me."

Luke was startled awake when two men shining flashlights opened the driver-side door.

"Why are you in my car?" Luke yelled.

Panicked, he turned on the ignition. One of the men grabbed Luke and pulled him away from the gearshift. The other man opened the passenger-side door and started to punch Luke in the face.

Luke's heart was racing as he struggled to get away.

One of the men jabbed Luke with a taser, sending 50,000 volts through his body. Luke continued to fight back.

BANG! BANG! The other man shot Luke in the chest, twice. *BANG!* Then he shot him a third time. Blood squirted from Luke's neck over the dashboard and windows, and soaked into the warm car seats where he had been sleeping.

Luke died at the scene.

Luke's mother sued the two police officers for wrongful death. Luke hadn't committed a crime. He did nothing wrong. The police officers assaulted *him*.

But a grand jury opted not to press charges against the officer for the fatal shooting, affirming the officer's rights to qualified immunity.

The "courts' approaches to police shootings are becoming increasingly deferential to police—and discounting facts that should require juries to decide whether or not police violated constitutional rights," the attorneys representing Luke's family said after the ruling, vowing to appeal the case.

***

References

1. https://www.reuters.com/investigates/special-report/usa-police-immunity-race/

2. https://www.cleveland.com/court-justice/2018/07/euclid_
   police_wins_lawsuit_fil.html
3. https://www.opn.ca6.uscourts.gov/opinions.
   pdf/20a0263p-06.pdf
4. https://www.cleveland.com/court-justice/2017/10/family_of_
   man_fatally_shot_by_1.html
5. https://www.cleveland.com/euclid/2017/08/what_absolved_
   euclid_police_of.html
6. https://www.lexipol.com/resources/blog/struggle-in-car-
   leads-to-deadly-shooting/

QUALIFIED IMMUNITY?

Dave Myers
Commander, San Diego Sheriff's Department, retired

In the wake of the Black Lives Matter protests during the summer of 2020, many Americans from all walks of life—including law enforcement officers—started to understand that many aspects of criminal justice in the United States required reexamination and greater scrutiny. One of the most significant issues that emerged from this soul searching was the concept of eliminating or modifying qualified immunity for law enforcement officers.

Ever since Congress passed the Civil Rights Act of 1871, individuals have had the right to sue state and local officials who violate their rights, including police officers. Over the past forty years, the United States Supreme Court has curtailed the right to sue public officials—especially police officers —based on the concerns that these individuals should not be penalized for conduct that was objectively reasonable and that frequent litigation could interfere with their work. The judicially created doctrine was conceived as a means of striking the proper balance between permitting compensation for the conduct of officials acting with ill motives, while not punishing those officers who, in good faith, did not know that their conduct would violate the constitutional rights of the plaintiff. The net result is that today, a police officer cannot be put on trial for using excessive force unless the person suing proves that:

1. The evidence shows or could convince a jury that the officer used excessive force; and
2. The officers should have known they were violating "clearly established" law, because a prior court case had already deemed similar police actions to be illegal.

What this has come to mean for victims of police violence is that even if a court finds that the officer used excessive force, it will grant immunity to police officers if the facts don't match an earlier case finding the same condut to be illegal. A special investigation conducted by Reuters found that this two-part standard makes it very difficult to hold police officers accountable for their actions. This is largely because courts are increasingly requiring a nearly identical case to use as precedent—and a court can almost always find or make up a factual difference between the case it's reviewing and an earlier case. In other words, given that each encounter with law enforcement is factually unique, courts do not need to resolve the issue of whether the conduct was indeed constitutional before concluding that the immunity applies.

Critics of qualified immunity believe that immunity standard has been applied so stringently that it is nearly impossible for courts to recognize even blatant examples of police misconduct as illegal. Take these cases:

- Outside of Dallas, Texas, five officers fired seventeen shots at a bicyclist who was 100 yards away, killing him, in a case of mistaken identity.
- In Heber City, Utah, an officer threw to the ground an unarmed man he had pulled over for a cracked windshield, leaving the man with brain damage.
- In Prince George's County, Maryland, an officer shot a man in a mental health crisis who was stabbing himself and trying to slit his own throat.

More recently, the courts granted immunity to Los Angeles County Sheriff's Department narcotics officers—including all nine members of an elite team—who in

February 2020 were charged with stealing more than $1.4 million in seized drug cash and using much of that money to buy homes, luxury cars, jewelry, and stocks. The officers' attorneys asserted—and the courts agreed—that because there was no exact precedent, the narcotics officers could not be expected to know that using more than $500,000 in stolen funds to buy cars, boats, homes, and other valuable assets was illegal.

Law enforcement's position on limiting or eliminating qualified immunity is that it is a necessary safe harbor in a fast-paced, often dangerous job. Police unions and law enforcement agencies argue that if the doctrine is eliminated to the point where there is no threshold and every case goes forward, police officers will start to hang back and avoid risky situations, even if it means criminal behavior goes unchallenged. They also predict that it will be harder to recruit enough officers without the protection of qualified immunity.

In my thirty-five-year law enforcement career, I can't recall two similar critical incidents I was ever involved in. In the heat of the moment, I brought to bear all of my training on tactics and the legal limits of my actions. I thought about what I needed to do to neutralize the public safety threat, what I needed to do to ensure that I would make it home that night, and what I could and could not do to address the situation that confronted me. Not once did

QUALIFIED IMMUNITY?

I think while handling the incidents, *Do I have qualified immunity if I do this?* or *Should I do this instead, since the facts of this situation match almost exactly a case that happened two years ago?*

Which brings us to my main point for why limiting qualified immunity is so important for any meaningful criminal justice reform, and for how we provide public safety in today's world.

The threats of lawsuits and holding police officers truly accountable for their actions will pressure their agencies and the people who lead them to properly train their officers, because in many agencies, training has not kept pace with the law enforcement needs of our communities. In addition to having to make split-second decisions on incomplete information with potentially life-or-death consequences, officers are required to handle medical emergencies, intervene in domestic-violence scenarios, and talk people through and out of crisis. Yet our training is shorter and less effective than for far less critical careers. In particular, while we are frequently called to deal with mentally ill individuals, few of us are trained to de-escalate confrontations with these individuals. Defusing conflict while minimizing the use of force requires building relationships proactively and employing proven de-escalation techniques, yet few academy or field training programs equip us with the power of these techniques. It should also be noted that limiting or eliminating qualified immunity will force agencies to be more transparent, by making them subject to discovery and depositions, which would not happen if the civil cases are not allowed to go forward. Yes, law enforcement will always have some "bad apples" for whom all the training in the world will not turn them into "good cops," but continuing to afford them the protection of qualified immunity for their egregiously wrong actions is antithetical to the rebuilding of community trust that is so badly needed at this time.

Dave Myers, a native San Diegan, retired from law enforcement after thirty-five years, working his way up the ranks from a patrol deputy to commander. He's worked in almost every part of the Sheriff's Department. He has authored several articles, including one on lone-wolf terrorism, LGBT in law enforcement, and regional law enforcement collaboration. Dave has served on several community youth-based service organizations. Currently he is a board member on two nonprofits, one supporting Gold Star Families and the other a legal impact community fund supporting criminal justice reform.

SEARCH AND STEAL

When Micah Jessop and Brittan Ashjian were served with a search warrant in 2013, they thought it was all a misunderstanding that would quickly be cleared up.

The two Fresno, California, businessmen were accused of illegal gambling and money laundering over two arcade games they had placed in retail stores.

"It's no different than the type of game you find at Chuck E. Cheese," Brittan insisted. The game involves the player trying to push quarters over a ledge to receive prizes.

Following the investigation, Micah and Brittan were not charged. But something unusual happened during the search.

The cops claimed they seized $50,000. But according to Micah and Brittan, the cops took $151,380 in cash and another $125,000 in rare and valuable coins.

Micah and Brittan filed a complaint with the city, but they never got their money back.

That's when they learned that one of the officers involved had been arrested by the feds for accepting a $20,000 bribe from a drug dealer. They became convinced that the officers booked $50,000 into evidence and pocketed the rest.

Micah and Brittan filed a lawsuit in 2015, but the courts did not help them. They gave the cops qualified immunity.

The Supreme Court has said that unless there's a clear precedent that police conduct was illegal in a similar situation, or unless the "violation is so obvious" that a precedent isn't needed, police should get qualified immunity.

In Micah and Brittan's case, the court concluded that the cops should get qualified immunity because they had acted on a valid search warrant, and "there was no clearly established law holding that officers violate the Fourth or Fourteenth Amendment when they steal property seized pursuant to a warrant."

The same judges who gave the officers qualified immunity acknowledged that "virtually every human society teaches that theft generally is morally wrong." But they added that "not all conduct that is improper or morally wrong, however, violates the Constitution."

"This is upsetting," Brittan said. "To know that if the police have a search warrant that's valid, they could steal your things and you don't have the ability to pursue it."

A number of civil liberties groups, including the Institute for Justice (IJ), offered to assist Micah and Brittan with their appeals when they learned about the case. Together, the groups worked with the two men and appealed all the way to the Supreme Court. Unfortunately, the Court declined to hear the case in 2020.

"The fundamental purpose of the Constitution and the Bill of Rights is to protect Americans from government abuses," said Anya Bidwell, an IJ attorney who represented Micah and Brittan. "But thanks to qualified immunity, police can literally come into your home and steal from you, and the courts will shield them from liability."

***

References

1. https://www.forbes.com/sites/nicksibilla/2020/05/13/should-cops-accused-of-stealing-over-225000-have-legal-immunity-supreme-court-urged-to-hear-case/?sh=a2bd69a28772

2. https://www.forbes.com/sites/nicksibilla/2019/09/17/federal-court-cops-accused-of-stealing-over-225000-have-legal-immunity/?sh=3c4b38515a85

3. https://www.fresnobee.com/news/local/article235405267.html

4. https://reason.org/wp-content/uploads/jessop-ashjian-v-city-of-fresno.pdf

5. http://cdn.ca9.uscourts.gov/datastore/
opinions/2019/09/04/17-16756.pdf (decision)

6. https://www.supremecourt.gov/
DocketPDF/19/19-1021/138419/20200317143611916_
39525%20pdf%20Gammon.pdf (SCOTUS AMICUS, IJ)

7. https://www.supremecourt.gov/
DocketPDF/19/19-1021/141481/20200413125515767_19%20
1021%20Motion%20for%20Leave%20to%20File%20
Amicus%20Brief.pdf (SCOTUS PETITION FOR CERT,
AMICUS)

8. https://www.supremecourt.gov/DocketPDF/
19/19-1021/141395/20200410160101121_Brief%20in%20
Opposition%20to%20Petition%20for%20Certiorari.pdf
(opposition to CERT from Fresno)

9. https://ij.org/wp-content/uplo
ads/2020/09/20200317143611916_39525-pdf-Gammon.pdf

10. https://ij.org/press-release/police-stole-225k-in-cash-and-
coins-and-the-courts-said-okay/

11. https://www.courthousenews.com/
judge-says-fresno-police-need-not-return-seized-items

12. https://newsmaven.io/pinacnews/eye-on-government/
california-cops-who-allegedly-stole-over-200-000-can-t-
be-sued-court-rules-Sv3PvkYVj0mz6hJOxFEXvg

BROKEN HOME

Six months pregnant with two young children in tow, Shaniz West returned home one afternoon to find five police officers with shotguns surveilling her house. They were looking for her ex-boyfriend, a gang member with outstanding warrants.

"May we have permission to go inside and apprehend him?" an officer asked.

"I don't think he's inside," Shaniz said, but she agreed to let the cops in.

She handed them the keys and then left with her children.

But the cops didn't use the keys. They called in a SWAT team, who bombarded the house with tear gas canisters. They shattered windows, kicked in the back door, and ransacked the house.

They tore through every room, smashing appliances, overturning furniture, knocking holes in the walls and the ceiling, and leaving behind toxic tear-gas residue all over Shaniz's family's possessions.

It looked like a "war zone," Shaniz later recalled.

Just as Shaniz had said, her ex-boyfriend wasn't there. The house was empty, except for Blue, the family dog, who survived the ordeal.

With nowhere for Shaniz and her children to stay, the city offered her $900 to cover the destruction of her belongings and three weeks in a hotel.

"It was grossly inadequate," her lawyer said. It was two months before her house was declared habitable again.

Shaniz sued the city and the officers. She wanted fair compensation. But she lost.

Since there was no previous case in which officers were found guilty of the exact same offense, the court granted them qualified immunity.

One judge dissented.

"It goes without saying that assaulting a home with tear gas and making the residential property uninhabitable for months is likewise unreasonable, and exceeds the scope of consent," the judge wrote.

The Institute for Justice learned about the case and offered to help Shaniz. They appealed to the Supreme Court, arguing that qualified immunity is a barrier to accountability and enables egregious police misconduct. But the Court decided not to hear the case. Justice Clarence

Thomas dissented from that decision, saying he wanted a chance to rethink qualified immunity.

***

References

1. https://www.forbes.com/sites/nicksibilla/2020/04/21/legal-loophole-gives-police-immunity-for-destroying-womans-home/?sh=231f7a5878d2
2. https://ij.org/case/west-v-city-of-caldwell/
3. https://www.idahopress.com/news/local/u-s-supreme-court-wont-hear-caldwell-womans-case-after-swat-team-damaged-her-home/article_d3e588bd-2369-50c3-8607-ae9c4b7226a4.html
4. https://www.courthousenews.com/cops-blast-house-instandoff-with-a-dog/
5. https://www.wsj.com/articles/tear-gas-grenades-and-qualified-immunity-11579133525
6. https://reason.com/2020/01/16/does-letting-police-enter-your-house-give-them-permission-to-wreck-it/

A MISGUIDED EXPERIMENT

Robert McNamara
The Institute For Justice

If you give government officials your consent to enter your home, does that mean they can instead destroy it by launching tear-gas grenades from the outside? If court rulings have said that government employees are not allowed to forcibly grope inmates and coworkers, does that mean a government-employed social worker can still forcibly grope his client? If the police are executing a warrant, does the Constitution allow them to just steal stuff for their own use instead of booking it into evidence?

These questions seem absurd. They *are* absurd. But even more absurd is the fact that the federal courts of appeal have answered each of these questions with a "yes"—or, at least, they have said that government officials cannot be punished for doing these things.

Outcomes like this are a direct result of qualified immunity, a rule that says government officials can only be held accountable for violating the Constitution if the constitutional rule they broke was "clearly established." And, in practice, "clearly established" means that a federal court has already held that exactly the same conduct in exactly the same circumstances violated the Constitution.

In other words, government officials have a free pass to violate your rights, as long as they manage to do so in a way no one has ever thought of before. So when the police took Shaniz West's permission to "get inside" her home as consent to destroy it with tear-gas grenades, it was not enough that the Supreme Court had already held that government officials may not exceed the scope of a property owner's consent to search. Instead, the officers in her case were entitled to qualified immunity because this exact situation had never come up before. There simply was no case in which police officers had interpreted permission to "get inside" a home as consent to destroy it from the sidewalk. Perhaps the question has never arisen because everyone understands that an invitation to come inside a home is not an invitation to destroy it from the sidewalk. (At least everyone I've ever invited into my home has understood this.) But for qualified immunity purposes, the reason does not matter. Instead, the sheer creativity of the government's argument meant that, at least for these officers, the Constitution just didn't apply that day.

And the bar for what counts as a sufficiently different constitutional violation can be shockingly low. Take Natia Sampson, who was assigned a government social worker as part of her attempt to adopt a troubled relative and who alleged that the social worker had sexually harassed and physically groped her. The Ninth Circuit acknowledged that it had already held that it was unconstitutional sex discrimination when a prison guard forcibly groped an inmate, and that it was unconstitutional sex discrimination when a government employee forcibly groped another government employee. But when a government employee groped a private citizen? There was no case to "clearly establish" whether that was okay, and so Ms. Sampson's constitutional claim was dead on arrival.

Nothing in the Constitution or federal statutes dictates these outcomes. Congress has never adopted a "one freebie" law when it comes to constitutional violations. Instead, the doctrine of qualified immunity is entirely a creation of the courts. Judges have simply decided, as a matter of policy, that government employees should be entitled to qualified immunity.

That policy was entirely an innovation of modern courts. It does not come from any longstanding legal principle. American courts have not historically asked whether a government official had violated "clearly established" law. Quite the contrary: Under the prevailing doctrines of the nineteenth century, a sheriff who wrongfully killed your cows or broke down your door was quite straightforwardly held liable for the damage he had caused.

And, like many innovations, qualified immunity has failed to fulfill its promises. It does not hold bad actors to account—the application of qualified immunity has nothing to do with how malicious (or, indeed, well-intentioned) a government official was. It does not reduce litigation costs—instead, it produces multiple rounds of appeals over whether rules were "clearly established" or not. It accomplishes little beyond making it harder to enforce the dictates of the Constitution—a document that was certainly never intended to be optional.

To be clear, reasonable people can and should disagree about what the Constitution means. Maybe it really was okay for law enforcement to destroy Shaniz West's house. Maybe it isn't unconstitutional sex discrimination when your social worker gropes you. There is a right answer to both of those questions, but these are debates all of us should be happy to have. Qualified immunity, though, has nothing to do with those debates. Instead, qualified immunity assumes the Constitution forbids whatever the government has done to a citizen and asks us to do nothing about it. In other words, qualified immunity commands that we look at government misconduct, acknowledge that it violates the Constitution, and then simply let it slide, because no prior case has exactly confronted these circumstances. That is a command at which principled people, both conservatives and liberals, rightly rebel. And it is past time for the misguided experiment with qualified immunity to end once and for all.

Robert McNamara is a senior attorney at the Institute for Justice, where he litigates cutting-edge constitutional cases protecting property rights, economic liberty, and other essential individual rights in both federal and state courts. In addition to litigation, his writing on legal issues has been published in The Wall Street Journal, The New York Times, The Washington Post, *and other outlets nationwide. In 2020, he led the team that represented Shaniz West in her quest to have the Supreme Court hold accountable the government officials who destroyed her home.*

WATCHING TV WHILE BLACK

"Where's the house?" Where we at? Where we at?" a deputy yelled into his radio.

Onree Norris, a seventy-eight-year-old Black man from Henry County, Georgia, was watching TV in his bedroom. When out of nowhere, *FLASH! BANG!* Something exploded in his living room.

His heart racing, Onree jumped out of bed and ran into the hallway. An army of black-armor-clad men with assault rifles ran toward him.

"On the ground!" a man yelled, grabbing Onree and hurling him to the ground, twisting his arm as if he were trying to snap it off and handcuffing him.

"Please," Ornee pleaded, "I just had heart surgery."

"Shut up!" the man yelled, holding him at gunpoint.

All around Onree, a cacophony of curses, as men tore his house apart.

It was a drug raid. But the SWAT team had the wrong house.

When the cops realized their mistake, they released Ornee and left. But by that point, the damage had been done.

The search warrant described the target house as off-white with a black roof. Onree's house—which was next door, with a separate driveway—was yellow with a gray roof. When the SWAT team arrived, a deputy had called in for confirmation, but never received a reply.

"Someone has to be held accountable for this," Wantez Robinson, Onree's grandson, said. "You should not be able to just go into someone's house because you feel like it."

"As a Black woman, it's like we are not valued as whole humans," LaCristy Johnson, Onree's granddaughter, said. "That's what it feels like. And I'm just wondering, what is it going to take for some people to see that?"

Onree sued the cops for violating his Fourth Amendment rights against unlawful search and seizure. But in March 2020, two years after the siege, a judge dismissed the complaint.

The judge was willing to concede that the officers had acted unlawfully. But, because a "clearly established" law had not been breached, the judge ruled that the officers were entitled to qualified immunity.

Now, at age eighty-one, Onree is currently appealing, in the hopes that a panel of judges reaches a different conclusion.

***

References

1. https://dockets.justia.com/docket/georgia/
   gandce/1:2018cv02163/250741
2. https://lawandcrime.com/crazy/georgia-cops-executed-no-
   knock-raid-on-the-wrong-house-and-a-78-year-old-man-a-
   judge-said-they-cant-be-sued/
3. https://www.king5.com/article/news/investigations/the-
   reveal/henry-county-no-knock-warrant-wrong-house/85-
   3af2b307-8a6a-4f8c-8355-3ebe58a8c508
4. https://www.msn.com/en-us/news/crime/its-like-we-
   are-not-valued-henry-county-family-sees-similarities-
   in-case-for-their-grandfather-breonna-taylor/
   ar-BB19ovcM
5. https://www.scribd.com/document/475572544/Federal-
   judge-grants-qualified-immunity-for-officers-that-raided-
   the-wrong-home
6. https://tenthamendmentcenter.com/2020/11/24/cops-
   terrorize-elderly-man-with-no-consequences-thanks-to-
   qualified-immunity/

TEDDY BEAR

Andrew Scott was a twenty-six-year-old "teddy bear," according to his longtime girlfriend, Miranda Mauck. He "was really good with the nerdy stuff" and enjoyed video games, building computers, and making people laugh.

Andrew and Miranda, both white, lived in an apartment complex in Leesburg, Florida. Andrew grew up around guns. His father, a correctional officer, taught him more than just how to handle a gun—he taught him to respect it.

Andrew legally owned a handgun and kept it locked in a safe in the apartment.

It was 1:30 a.m. *BOOM, BOOM, BOOM.* Someone was pounding on their door. Andrew and Miranda threw their clothes on. *BOOM, BOOM, BOOM.* The knocking continued. Andrew grabbed his gun from the safe.

Andrew opened the door with one hand, holding the gun pointed to the ground in his other hand.

A police officer pushed into the apartment. Gunshots split the air. *BANG! BANG! BANG!*

"They shot me!" Adrew cried out. "They fucking shot me. I'm dying!"

Blood pooled around him on the floor. Andrew was dead, shot six times at point blank.

The officer had tailed a suspect to the apartment complex, but had come to the wrong apartment. The cops detained Miranda, locking her in the patrol car for hours.

"They didn't even say anything," Miranda recalled later. The police never identified themselves.

Andrew's family and Miranda sued the cops, but the trial judge refused to let a jury decide the case, granting the officers qualified immunity.

Miranda and Andrew's family, with the support of legal advocacy groups, kept fighting.

They took their case all the way to the Supreme Court. But the Court declined the case.

Meanwhile, after an investigation, the officer who killed Andrew was allowed to return to active duty without facing discipline.

***

References

1. https://kfgo.com/2020/11/20/special-report-when-cops-and-americas-cherished-gun-rights-clash-cops-win/

2. https://graphics.thomsonreuters.com/
   srepfiles/2020/qi-three-master/en/pdf/
   statepoliceinvestigationintoAndrewScottdeath.pdf
3. https://thecrimereport.org/2020/11/20/
   how-immunity-helps-cops-win-excessive-force-suits/
4. https://www.nejamelaw.com/news/i-demand-justice-for-
   my-son.html
5. https://www.reuters.com/investigates/special-report/
   usa-police-immunity-guns/
6. https://graphics.thomsonreuters.com/
   srepfiles/2020/qi-three-master/en/pdf/
   Youngvbordersappealscourtdecision.pdf
7. https://graphics.thomsonreuters.com/srepfiles/2020/
   qi-three-master/en/pdf/YoungvBordersappealscourtruling.
   pdf
8. https://graphics.thomsonreuters.com/srepfiles/2020/
   qi-three-master/en/pdf/prosecutorScottshootingmemo.pdf

NO ONE IS ABOVE THE LAW

Julia Yoo

A fundamental tenet of our system of governance is that no one is above the law—both King and Pauper must adhere to the same set of rules. But qualified immunity erodes the principle of equal enforcement of laws. It destroys community trust and creates the perception of a two-track system of power: Police officers are permitted to act with impunity, while the communities they police are victimized with no recourse and no forum to vindicate their rights. Qualified immunity, eating away at our Constitutional rights, sends a clear message to victims of police misconduct: Law enforcement officers are above the law.

When a member of the community is victimized, there are only three ways in which a sense of justice and equity can be restored: criminal charges against the officer, internal discipline, and civil justice. Criminal charges against police officers are rare. We saw that with the killings of Michael Brown, Eric Garner, Tamir Rice, Stephon Clark, and Breonna Taylor. In the rare case where charges are brought, officers are frequently acquitted, as we saw in the criminal prosecution of the officers involved in the killings of Freddie Gray and Philando Castile.

As to internal investigations, there are 18,000 non-federal policing agencies in the United States, and no uniform standards in policing, written policies and procedures, performance standards, and reviews or reporting. Each agency sets its own policies for investigation and discipline. Discipline proceedings are almost never transparent, and meaningful discipline is rare. This is the backdrop in which victims of police misconduct are told the door to civil justice is closed to them.

In June 2020, the Supreme Court announced it would decline to hear any of the cases pending before it on qualified immunity, leaving aggrieved victims of police violence without hope of justice or accountability. One of those cases was *Jessop v. City of Fresno*, in which the victim alleged that officers stole more than $225,000 in cash and rare coins during a search of his home. The Ninth Circuit noted that the act was "morally wrong," but protected the officers from suit by granting qualified immunity, because the court had not previously held that stealing property during an otherwise authorized search was a constitutional violation. Worse still, *Jessop* refused to hold that stealing cash and gold coins violates the Constitution, meaning officers stealing during execution of a search warrant will still escape civil liability under qualified immunity.

This is a direct result of *Pearson v. Callahan*, 555 U.S. 223 (2009), in which the Court eradicated the requirement that courts first adjudicate whether the official's conduct violated the Constitution. As a result, district courts now grant qualified immunity without ever deciding whether a constitutional violation occurred in the first instance, creating a never-ending loop of constitutional violations. Victims cannot seek civil justice against officers who harmed them because the harmful conduct has not been "clearly established," but because so many cases are dismissed without the court addressing whether the challenged conduct was a violation, it never becomes established. Cases like *Jessop* create constitutional stagnation, where the jurisprudence is never established, continuing to excuse the most egregious misconduct. This is particularly troubling in the advent of new technologies in weaponry, where there can be no prior case addressing the constitutional limits of the new weapons, even though the wrong is obvious.

Such was the case in 2005 when Carl Bryan, whose only crime was a seatbelt violation, was tasered by a Coronado,

California, police officer. Carl froze and fell forward, knocking out his front teeth. Carl had posed no threat and was wearing only boxer shorts and shoes. Tasers were a relatively new weapon in 2005, with officers using the weapon on children, pregnant women, people standing in water, people who had committed only traffic infractions, the elderly, the disabled, and people on bicycles. We litigated this case for four years. Ultimately, the Ninth Circuit held that the use of the taser in these circumstances violated the Constitution, but because there was no prior case addressing the propriety of the use of the taser, and dismissed the case based on qualified immunity. While this case was pending, departments across the country continued to taser people indiscriminately, having been told by the manufacturer that this "non-lethal" weapon was a safe alternative that did not harm people. It was only after four years of hard-fought litigation in *Bryan v. MacPherson* that departments across the country were forced to evaluate their policies. Unlike *Jessop*, we were at least victorious in establishing a new law and halting dangerous taser practices that were causing catastrophic injuries and deaths. The power and the impact of civil rights litigation is not felt only by the victims themselves. Seeking civil justice is a vindication of the rights of all people when the litigants fight for institutional changes.

Those who argue the elimination of qualified immunity would have limited consequences on officer conduct have ignored the realities of policing. In a case involving the death of a schizophrenic patient in a San Diego jail, the grieving parents discovered that the jail officials did not start an investigation into their son's death until a newspaper published an article about the lawsuit. But for filing a case, their son's death would have gone unnoticed and uninvestigated. This case resulted in changes in the medical information gathering and resulted in the termination of the private company that provided medical services to the county jails.

But at what cost do we establish the contours of our rights? Qualified immunity has a chilling effect on victims of misconduct and their attorneys. Civil rights attorneys are less inclined each year to bear the increasing risk of spending four to six years and tens of thousands of dollars in litigation expenses, only to have the case thrown out. Even without qualified immunity, the threshold for establishing that a particular conduct violated the Constitution is exceedingly high. The sheer difficulty of winning discourages most lawyers from pursuing a case. Even when victims can find attorneys willing to take the risk, they are forced to carry a heavy burden, subjecting themselves to scrutiny and a lengthy and perilous legal process.

The price of qualified immunity is not only paid by the victims of police misconduct and their advocates. In addition to eroding any sense of equity in our communities of color, immunities also harm police officers who enter the profession with a true sense of purpose to serve the public. Immunities take away the public trust and confidence that is critical for officer safety and effective policing. When the community believes that officers literally get away with murder and theft, the badge they carry has no honor. Immunities create a toxic environment of community distrust. Undoing the harm of qualified immunity is one step, but a significant step, toward true transformation of the system of racial inequality and restoration of community faith in our justice system.

Julia Yoo is a partner with Iredale & Yoo in San Diego, California. She is President of the National Police Accountability Project and a member of the Board of Governors of the Consumer Attorneys of California.

HOME, SWEET HOME

Shase Howse was just returning home from the store when he heard a voice behind him. He was talking with his mom on the phone and fumbling with his keys.

"Do you live here?" a man asked.

"Yes, this is my house," Shase replied. "I live here."

Shase, a twenty-year-old Black man and self-described homebody, looked behind him and saw three white men in a vehicle.

"Do you live here?" the man asked again.

"Yes. This is my home. What the fuck?" Shase said.

"You have a smart mouth and a bad attitude," the man said.

Shase turned back toward his house as the man continued to jabber on about his "smart mouth." The man got out of the car.

"Put your hands behind your back," he said. "You're going to jail." The other two men got out of the car.

Shase was confused. He hadn't done anything wrong. He was just coming home from the store.

The man lunged at Shase, tackling him to the ground.

Shase's mother, Nicholasa Santari, rushed home to find the three strangers on her porch, one of them beating up her son. She watched, helplessly, as the man struck Shase twice in the back of the neck with his fist. Nicholasa begged him to stop.

The officers handcuffed Shase, charged him with assault, and dragged him to jail, where he spent two nights before his mother posted bond. The man who accosted Shase was a plainclothes detective who had not identified himself. He later testified that he and the other officers had approached Shase because they saw him "milling about" what they believed to be an abandoned house. They thought he was "taking too long to open the door," that he seemed "nervous, glancing back and forth."

The charges against Shase were dropped. Then Shase and his attorney, James Hardiman, filed a lawsuit, alleging that the officers had maliciously prosecuted Shase and used excessive force, violating his Fourth Amendment rights.

The court granted all three cops qualified immunity and threw the case out.

"Mr. Howse had to present a case where a court had ruled that an officer acting under similar circumstances had violated the Fourth Amendment," the court stated. "Without such a case, the plaintiff will always lose."

Not all the judges agreed with the ruling, however. In her dissent, Justice Julia Smith Gibbons wrote, "In framing Shase Howse's right in this case, the panel fails to account for his suspected criminality (none), location (home), or conduct (truthfully answering questions)."

Backed by the NAACP, Hardiman filed a petition on Shase's behalf in 2020 to argue his case in front of the Supreme Court, where it awaits a decision as to whether the justices will hear the case.

Previously, despite calls from the Supreme Court's most conservative justice (Clarence Thomas) and one of its most liberal ones (Sonia Sotomayor) to revisit qualified immunity, the majority of the Court has refused to do so.

***

References

1. https://www.cleveland.com/metro/2017/07/lawsuit_claims_cleveland_offic_1.html
2. https://casetext.com/case/howse-v-hodous
3. https://www.reuters.com/article/usa-police-immunity-race/special-report-challenging-police-violence-while-black-idINL1N2J00GT
4. https://www.davisvanguard.org/2020/12/naacp-petition-to-supreme-court-revives-debate-over-use-of-qualified-immunity-for-police/

5. https://www.pfaw.org/blog-posts/trump-judge-excuses-police-brutality-without-trial-confirmed-judges-confirmed-fears/

6. https://www.opn.ca6.uscourts.gov/opinions.pdf/20a0177p-06.pdf

TWO-WHEELING

It was early Saturday morning when gunshots and sirens rang out in rural Kaufman County, Texas. Gabriel Winzer, a twenty-five-year-old, developmentally disabled Black man, heard the commotion and wanted to see what was happening.

He threw on his blue jacket, stuffed a bright orange toy cap gun in his waistband, hopped on his bicycle, and pedaled down the road.

Gabriel's friends described him as "kind to everyone he came in contact with." He was a college graduate, a loving uncle, and a polite, "well-behaved kid."

Meanwhile, five police officers were on the scene, responding to reports of an erratic man on foot kicking mailboxes and shooting a pistol.

BANG! Another shot fired. The officers could see the suspect about 100 yards away, wearing a brown shirt and blue jeans. Then he disappeared into the trees on foot. The officers moved down the road at a distance, taking cover behind their vehicles.

"Stay indoors," the officers instructed curious residents and onlookers.

That's when they saw Gabriel on his bicycle 100 yards away.

"Drop your weapon!" the officers yelled. Then they opened fire.

The rattling of gunshots split the air. The cops fired at least seventeen shots, hitting Gabriel four times. He fell off his bike and stumbled into his family's backyard. His father, Henry, ran out to help.

The police handcuffed Gabriel, tasing him as he resisted. Henry tried to help. The cops tased him, too.

Gabriel went limp. He was pronounced dead at the scene from the gunshot wounds.

Claiming that Henry tried to bite them, the officers arrested him for "aggravated assault with a deadly weapon." Henry was convicted by an all-white jury.

Gabriel's death rocked the community. "There were no seats left in the church" for Gabriel's funeral, a friend recalled. "The aisles were filled with people standing shoulder to shoulder, the lobby was full, the front doors were propped open and people spilled out onto the sidewalk outside."

But one person was missing the day of the funeral: Gabriel's father.

Gabriel's mother sued the county and the police officers.

The appeals court ruled that the lawsuit against Kaufman County should proceed, that a jury should get to decide whether Gabriel's constitutional rights were violated. But the jury sided with the cops, granting them qualified immunity, and threw out the case against them.

***

A PERVERSE IRONY

Ben Cohen

PROBLEM

In 1871, shortly after the end of the United States Civil War, Congress recognized a growing crisis for post-slavery Reconstruction: police and other public servants were discriminating against and brutalizing Black people.

SOLUTION

To address it, Congress passed a series of laws that came to be known as the Ku Klux Klan Acts—a reference to the fact that many of those police and public servants were members of the Klan. Officially titled the Civil Rights Act of 1871, the law provides that a person who was discriminated against or brutalized could sue the public employee who broke the law by violating their rights.

The Act states that if a public official violates your constitutional rights—your protection against unlawful search and seizure, your protection against cruel and unusual punishment, your protection against unlawful detention—you are allowed to sue that public official, holding them *financially* accountable for their conduct. The language is not ambiguous. "*Every*" state official who causes a "deprivation of *any rights*" guaranteed by the Constitution and its laws "shall be *liable to the party injured.*"

At first, the Supreme Court applied this law as it was written.

EVISCERATION

But in a series of decisions from 1967 to 1982, the Supreme Court gutted the Ku Klux Klan Act by creating out of whole cloth the legal defense of qualified immunity.

So, here's how it works today: An officer who violates someone's constitutional rights will generally be protected from suit unless the victim can identify previous judicial opinions that addressed the specific context and conduct. This is very far afield from what Congress sought to achieve in the Civil Rights Act. Instead of considering whether a person's civil rights have been violated, courts shut their eyes to whether a crime has been committed and look only to see if there has been a past conviction of a police officer for doing the exact same thing. Otherwise, it gets thrown out of court.

And then there's the Catch-22. If you can only bring a case to trial if there's already been a precedent for an exactly identical case, how do you create a new precedent? You can't. In legal jargon, the law is "frozen."

This is a perverse irony. A law meant to protect blacks from capricious state action has now evolved through judicial interpretation into a law that makes capricious state action less likely to face sanction. A law that makes no mention of immunity is now somehow used as the basis for providing police immunity.

—*San Diego Star Tribune*

CONTINUING PROBLEM

The law to combat white supremacist police officers was eviscerated; yet police departments across our country have continued to be infiltrated by white supremacist officers.

In 1964, Freedom Summer, investigators discovered the scattered remains of eight college students in and around the town of Philadelphia, Mississippi. Several of the students were members of CORE, the Congress of Racial Equality, who were helping Black people register to vote. Four of the Klansmen charged with the kidnapping and killing of the students were current or former police officers.

Even into the 1970s, many states beyond the Deep South maintained what were called "sundown towns," towns and larger municipalities where police officers, vigilante mobs, and others enforced official and quasi-official policies prohibiting Black and other nonwhite people from remaining in town past sunset. These were not isolated incidents. In fact, there were an estimated 10,000 "sundown towns" across the United States.

In the 1980s, a Jefferson County, Kentucky, police officer was exposed as a Klan leader during the statewide investigation of a Ku Klux Klan firebombing of a Black couple's home in the previously all-white neighborhood of Sylviana. In a deposition, the officer, Alex Young, admitted to heading a Klan-affiliate with forty members called COPS (Confederate Officers Patriot Squad), more than half of whom were local law enforcement officers. Not only was Young's role in the KKK *known* to this police department, it was tolerated—so long as he agreed not to publicize it.

In the 1990s, residents in the town of Lynwood, California, filed a class action lawsuit against a gang of racist LA County sheriff's deputies (known as the "Lynwood Vikings") for carrying out "systematic acts of shooting, killing, brutality, terrorism, house-trashing and other acts of lawlessness and wanton abuse of power." A federal judge overseeing the case labeled the Lynwood Vikings "a neo-Nazi, white supremacist gang" that carried out racist attacks and intimidation against the Black and Latino communities in LA County.

In 1996, the county was forced to pay $9 million in civil rights settlements. In 2019, following the shooting of an unarmed Black man by two sheriff's deputies, LA County had to pay $7 million more to settle a wrongful death lawsuit after testimony revealed that the deputies were part of a group of officers with matching tattoos "in the tradition of earlier deputy gangs." In fact, nearly sixty lawsuits against alleged members of deputy gangs have cost the county about $55 million, "which includes $21 million in cases over the last 10 years."

In 2001, two Texas sheriff's deputies were fired after they exposed their KKK affiliation in an attempt to recruit other officers.

Between 2009 and 2014, three different cops in Fruitland Park, Florida, were fired or chose to resign after their Klan memberships were exposed.

In 2009, city officials in Anniston, Alabama, discovered that one of the city officers was a member of the League of the South, a secessionist, neo-Confederate white nationalist organization. The police chief, knowing this, decided that the officer's membership in such an organization had no impact on his job performance. The officer was allowed to remain on the job, eventually enjoying promotions to sergeant and lieutenant on the force. Only in 2015, after the Southern Poverty Law Center uncovered the language of a speech this officer had given at a League of the South conference (in which he described recruiting other law enforcement officers to the organization), did his department relieve him of his duties.

In 2015, a Louisiana cop was removed from the force after a picture surfaced showing him extending the Nazi salute at a KKK anti-immigration rally at an undisclosed location in North Carolina.

In 2017, Colbert, Oklahoma, police chief Bart Alsbrook resigned in shame after local media reported his decades-long involvement with skinhead groups and his ownership and active management of two neo-Nazi websites. Just one year later, the nearby city of Achille, Oklahoma, confirmed that Alsbrook had been hired as a reserve officer in its police department.

In 2018, a police chief in Greensboro, Maryland, pleaded guilty for forging documentation to hire an officer who had previously been forced to resign from the Dover, Delaware, police department for assaulting a Black man and fracturing his jaw. That same officer, Thomas Webster IV, was later involved in the death of an unarmed Black teenager. The subsequent investigation revealed twenty-nine "use of force" reports at his previous job, including some that were deemed unnecessary uses of force. These previous incidents were never reported to the Maryland police certification board prior to Webster's hiring.

As recently as June 2020, three Wilmington, North Carolina, officers were fired for using racial epithets on camera, including using racial slurs to describe the magistrate and police chief. They joked about shooting Black people, including one of their fellow police officers. One cop shared his eagerness for martial law so that he could go out and "slaughter" Black people.

A month later, four cops in San Jose, California, were suspended pending investigation into their membership and participation in a Facebook group that regularly posted racist and Islamaphoic material. Seeing a post about the summer-long Black Lives Matter protests across the country, one officer allegedly responded, "Black lives really don't matter."

January 6, 2021—at least 20 police officers from around the country have been charged or are under investigation for the invasion of the United States Capitol building, which was marked by confederate white supremacist overtones.

RE-SOLUTION

To say that the only people who we give the privilege to use lethal force in our name should not be held accountable is a travesty. To say that the people we employ to uphold the law are above the law is tyranny.

If I shoot someone or beat someone up or steal or destroy someone's house for no good reason, I am liable.

To say that if I put on a police uniform and get paid to do it, then I'm not liable, is outrageous.

We can do this.
We can get this right.
IF we decide to do it.
If YOU decide to do it.
Qui
He who is silent consents.

Ben Cohen
Co-founder, Ben & Jerry's
Team member, Campaign to End Qualified Immunity

Visit the **Campaign to End Qualified Immunity** website at CampaignToEndQualifiedImmunity.org and sign up to help, or send an email to CTEQI@PeoplePowerInitiatives.org and say you'd like to help.

PLAYERS COALITION
LETTER

June 10, 2020

Dear Members of the United States Congress:

We are more than 1,400 current and former professional athletes and coaches from across the National Football League, National Basketball Association, and Major League Baseball in America. We are tired of conversations around police accountability that go nowhere, and we have engaged in too many "listening sessions" where we discuss whether there is a problem of police violence in this country. There *is* a problem. The world witnessed it when Officer Chauvin murdered George Floyd, and the world is watching it now, as officers deploy enormous force on peaceful protestors like those who were standing outside of the White House last week. The time for debate about the unchecked authority of the police is over; it is now time for change.

We are writing to ask that you pass the bill to end qualified immunity introduced by Representatives Justin Amash and Ayanna Pressley. Congress passed the Ku Klux Klan Act in 1871 to give ordinary citizens recourse when powerful public officials violate constitutional rights. By passing that act, codified in 42 U.S.C. 1983, Congress told its citizenry that no one is above the law, especially those who abuse government power. A healthy democracy requires no less; citizens must know that if those who promise to uphold the law and protect the community fail to do so, there is a remedy available. The law, as one author has noted, is "a bulwark of American liberty."

The Supreme Court has caused irreparable harm to public trust by creating and then expanding the doctrine of qualified immunity, which often exempts police officers and others from liability, even for shocking abuse. Under that doctrine, first developed in 1967 and widened ever since, plaintiffs must show that government officials violated "clearly established" law to receive damages for harm. A plaintiff wins only if a prior court found an official liable under a nearly identical fact-pattern. This standard is virtually impossible to meet, and the protections promised under section 1983 seem largely symbolic as a result.

Qualified immunity has shielded some of the worst law enforcement officials in America. The Eighth Circuit applied it to an officer who wrapped a woman in a bear hug, slammed her to the ground, and broke her collarbone as she walked away from him. The Ninth Circuit applied the doctrine to two officers who allegedly stole $225,000 while executing a search warrant. The Eleventh Circuit applied the doctrine to protect an officer who unintentionally shot a ten-year-old while firing at the family dog (who, much like the child, posed no threat). The list of officers who suffered no consequences because of this doctrine could fill a law book.

It is time for Congress to eliminate qualified immunity, and it can do so by passing the Amash-Pressley bill. When police officers kill an unarmed man, when they beat a woman, or when they shoot a child, the people of this country must have a way to hold them accountable in a court of law. And officers must know that if they act in such a manner, there will be repercussions. A legal system that does not provide such a recourse is an illegitimate one. In their grief, people have taken to the streets because, for too long, their government has failed to protect them. The Courts and elected officials alike have instead shielded people who caused unspeakable harm. Congress must not be complicit in these injustices, and it should take this important step to show that law enforcement abuse will not be tolerated.

Sincerely,

Players Coalition members, current/former NFL, NBA, MLB players and coaches:

Ameer Abdullah
Matthew Adams
Rodney Adams
Klayton Adams
Sam Adams
Josh Adams
Quincy Adeboyejo
Jude Adjei-
  Barimah
  McTelvin Agim
Chidi Ahanotu
Eric Alexander
Anthony Alford
Raul Allegre
Beau Allen
Ian Allen
Dakota Allen
Josh Allen
Ricardo Allen
Bennie Anderson
Charlie Anderson
Tim Anderson
David Andrews
Marty Anthony-
  Lyons Kenny
  Anunike
Chris Archer
Terron Armstead
Jessie Armstead
Arik Armstead
Amon Arnold
Dan Audick
Denico Autry
Brendon
  Ayanbadejo
  Obafemi
  Ayanbadejo
  Stevie Baggs Jr.
Robert Bailey
Kabeer
  Baja-Biamila
Brian Baker
Doug Baldwin
David Ball
Larry Ball
Carl Banks
Tony Banks
Ben Banogu
Shawn Barber
Luq Barcoo

Kenjon Barner
Erich Barnes
Ben Bartch
Essang Bassey
Daren Bates
Nick Bawden
Gary Baxter
Jarrod Baxter
Kelvin Beachum
Chris Beake
Tim Beckham
Odell Beckham Jr.
Greg Bell
Kurt Benkert
Bene Benwikere
Alex Bregman
Damien Berry
Justin Bethel
McLeod Bethel-
  Thompson Eric
  Bieniemy
Adam Bighill
Andrew Billings
Joel Bitonio
Julian Blackmon
Ronald Blair
Matt Blanchard
Rodrigo
  Blankenship
Jeff Bleamer
Joe Bleymaier
Dennis Bligen
David Blough
CJ Board
Joe Bock
Kim Bokamper
Juran Bolden
Victor Bolden
Anquan Boldin
Ron Bolton
Rik Bonness
Jon Borchardt
Dave Borgonzi
A.J. Bouye
Dwayne Bowe
Tom Brady
Marcus Brady
Mark Brammer
Colin Branch
Marcelis Branch

Delvin Breaux
Drew Brees
Sam Brenner
Michael Brewster
Lamont Brightful
Dezmon Briscoe
Jacoby Brissett
Derrick Brooks
Chet Brooks
Ethan Brooks
Terrence Brooks
Trent Brown
Eric Brown
Milford Brown
Evan Brown
Chris Brown
Kris Brown
Donald Brown
Terell Brown
Travis Bruffy
Austin Bryant
DJ Bryant
Corbin Bryant
Armonty Bryant
DeForest Buckner
Daniel Bullocks
Jarrod Bunch
Ian Bunting
Oren Burks
Jason Burns
Jeff Burris
Derrick Burroughs
Noah Burroughs
Joe Burrow
Deante Burton
Jermon Bushrod
Vernon Butler
LeRoy Butler
Rashad Butler
Victor Butler
Demetrius Butler
  Sr.
Byron Buxton
Kevin Byard
Keith A. Byars
Israel Byrd
Erik C. McMillan
Shilique Calhoun
Chris Calloway
Greg Camarillo

PLAYERS COALITION LETTER

Parris Campbell
Calais Campbell
Khary Campbell
Tommie Campbell
Sheldon Canley
AJ Cann
Stephen Carlson
Chris Carter
Ron'Dell Carter
Tony Carter
Gerald Carter
Jim Carter
Jamal Carter
Jurrell Casey
Jonathan Casillas
Jehuu Caulcrick
Dan Chamberlain
Chris Chambers
Kam Chancellor
Wes Chandler
Sean Chandler
Steve Christie
Bradley Chubb
Ryan Clady
Bruce Clark
Darion Clark
Will Clarke
Adrian Clayborn
Chris Claybrooks
Mark Clayton
Nate Clements
Tyrie Cleveland
Steve Clifford
Kameron Cline
Randall Cobb
Kendall Coleman
Andre Coleman
Henry Coley IV
Jedidiah Collins
Mark Collins
Jalen Collins
Marques Colston
Chuck Commiskey
Jack Conklin
Albert Connell
Dan Connor
Curtis Conway
Toi Cook
Logan Cooke
Brayden Coombs

Stephen Cooper
Chris Cooper
Amari Cooper
Russell Copeland
Doug Costin
Mark Cotney
Ted Cottrell
Nathan Cottrell
John Covington
Christian
  Covington
  Dameyune Craig
James Crawford
Tre Crawford
JP Crawford
Jack Crawford
Joe Cribbs
Chuck Crist
Marcus Cromartie
JC Cross
AJ Cruz
Lloyd
  Cushenberry
  III Jonathan
  Cyprien
Carl D. Howard Jr.
  Brendan Daly
Eugene Daniel
Owen Daniels
Joe Danna
Matt Darby
Najeh Davenport
Tae Davis
Demario Davis
Carlton Davis
Todd Davis
Tyrone Davis
Eric Davis
Billy Davis
Oliver Davis
Travis Davis
Davion Davis
John Davis
Sammy Davis
Tony Davis
Tyler Davis
Akeem Davis
Ryan Davis Sr.
Dion Dawkins

Lawrence Dawsey
  Keyunta Dawson
Sheldon Day
Fred Dean
Joe DeCamillis
Travis Demeritte
Anthony Denman
Delino DeShields
  Jr.
Pierre Desir
Ian Desmond
Toderick Devoe
Korey
  Diede-Jones
Na'il Diggs
AJ Dillon
Josh Dobbs
Andrew Donnal
Kevin Dotson
Jamil Douglas
Marcus Dowdell
Jack Doyle
Tyronne
  Drakeford
Pete Draovitch
Troy Drayton
Davon Drew
Jack Driscoll
Clifton Duck
Rickey Dudley
Bill Duff
Bobby Duhon
Ashton Dulin
Michael Dumas
JoLonn Dunbar
Jamie Duncan
Keldrick Dunn
Justin Dunn
Keith Dunn
Jon Duplantier
Tim Dwight
Jeffrey E Faulkner
Michael Early
Jacob Eason
Matt Eberflus
Samson Ebukam
Dwan Edwards
David Edwards
Emeke Egbule
Jake Eldrenkamp

ABOVE THE LAW

Bruce Elia
Keith Elias
Ben Ellefson
Emmanuel
  Ellerbee
Porter Ellett
Jake Elliot
Greg Ellis
Justin Ellis
Elbert Ellis
Percy Ellsworth
Jermaine
  Eluemunor
Jon Embree
Larry English
Zach Ertz
Jordan Evans
Demetric Evans
Nate Evans
Darrynton Evans
Harry F. Sydney III
Zane Fakes
Vic Fangio
Wes Farnsworth
James Farrior
Jeffrey Faulkner
Marlon Favorite
Tavien Feaster
Nick Ferguson
Prince Fielder
Yamon Figurs
John Fina
Dave Fiore
Tony Fisher
Jack Flaherty
Timothy Flanders
Brian Fleury
Drayton Florence
  Christopher
  Foerster
Drew Forbes
Bernard Ford
Daurice Fountain
Melvin Fowler
Dexter Fowler
Vernon Fox
Eric Frampton
Zaire Franklin
Byron Franklin
Parks Frazier

Mike Frazier
Kavon Frazier
Dwight Freeney
Eddie Fuller
Jedidiah G Collins
  Christian Gaddis
Russell Gage
Russell Gage
William Gaines
EJ Gaines
Joel Gamble
Jonathan Gannon
Malik Gant
Kenneth Gant
Mark Garalczyk
Jim Garcia
Dr. Leonard
  Garrett
Myles Garrett
Amir Garrett
Rashan Gary
Percell Gaskins
Jordan Gay
Shaun Gayle
Tony George
Nathan Gerry
Antonio Gibson
Tony Gilbert
Joe Giles-Harris
Nate Gilliam
Reginald Gipson
Jordan Glasgow
Graham Glasgow
La'Roi Glover
Terry Godwin
Keith Goganious
Nick Goings
Tony Gonzalez
Julian
  Good-Jones
Donald Goode
Niko Goodrum
Marquise
  Goodwin
CJ Goodwin
Melvin Gordon
Dee Gordon
Melvin Gordon
Colby Gossett
Jermaine Grace

Earnest Graham
Devin Gray
Chaz Green
Farrod Green
Gerri Green
Ahman Green
Willie Green
Ethan Greenidge
Jabari Greer
Steve Gregory
Nick Greisen
Michael Griffin
Otis Grigsby
Jordan Gross
Tori Gurley
Lawrence Guy
Myron Guyton
Jalen Guyton
Tony Gwynn Jr.
John Hagg
Dennis Haley
Grant Haley
Bryan Hall
PJ Hall
Adrian Hamilton
Davon Hamilton
Antonio Hamilton
Jakar Hamilton
Josh Hammond
William Hampton
Justin Hardy
Sean Harlow
Wade Harman
Duron Harmon
Roman Harper
Tobias Harris
DeMichael Harris
Erik Harris
Chris Harris
Deonte Harris
Jonathan Harris
Josh Harrison
John Harty
Willie Harvey
Willie Harvey Jr.
Sam Havrilak
DJ Hayden
Ke'bryan Hayes
Alex Haynes
Johnny L. Hector

PLAYERS COALITION LETTER

Gene Heeter
Johnny Hekker
Thomas
  Henderson
  Othello
  Henderson
Amari Henderson
Malik Henry
Mario Henry
Mo Henry
Drew Henson
Tre Herndon III
Reggie Herring
Mark Herzlich
Jason Heyward
Clifford Hicks
Jordan Hicks
Mike Hiestand
Rashard Higgins
Dont'a Hightower
Richard
  Hightower
Rajon Hill
Anthony Hill
Efrem Hill
Brian Hill
Dontrell Hilliard
Ronnie Hillman
TY Hilton
Brandon Hitner
Liffort Hobley
Alijah Holder
Johnny Holland
Justin Hollins
Torry Holt
Robert Holt
Rolland Hooks
Austin Hooper
Bob Horn
Bobby Howard
Rich Howell
Brian Hoyer
Chris Hubbard
Orlando Hudson
Tyrone Hughes
John Hughes
Dante Hughes
Daymeion Hughes
Charley Hughlett
Akeem Hunt

Tony Hunter
Earnest Hunter
Wayne Hunter
Allen Hurns
Jalen Hurts
Von Hutchins
Sidney Hy
  Abramowitz
  Duke Ihenacho
Ken Irvin
Kemal Ishmael
Corey Ivy
Steven Jackson
Darius Jackson
Honor Jackson
Maurice Jackson
Ray Jackson
Malik Jackson
Austin Jackson
Leon Jacobs
Kendyl Jacox
Ja'Wuan James
Jeno James
Quentin Jammer
Mike Jasper
Jim Jeffcoat
Malik Jefferson
Roy Jefferson
Willie Jefferson
Jegs Jegede
Malcolm Jenkins
Ronney Jenkins
Jarvis Jenkins
Rashad Jennings
Jim Jensen
Josey Jewell
William
Joe Jackson
Marcus Johnson
Fulton Johnson
Travis Johnson
Joe Johnson
Jesse Johnson
Collin Johnson
A.J. Johnson
Sherman Johnson
Isaiah Johnson
Will Johnson
Nico Johnson

Cameron
  Johnston
Sidney Jones
Dominique Jones
Robbie Jones
Garrick Jones
Donald Jones
Brian Jones
Charlie Jones
Abry Jones
Charles Jones
Joe Jones
Deion Jones
JT Jones
Bennie Joppru
Cameron Jordan
James Jordan
Karl Joseph
Sebastian Joseph-
  Day Yonel
  Jourdain
Cato June
Luke Juriga
Kyle Juszczyk
Ryan K. Russell
Kevin Kaesviharn
Mike Kafka
John Kaiser
ND Kalu
Alvin Kamara
Jevon Kearse
Frank Kearse
Khaylan Kearse-
  Thomas Case
  Keenum
Keone Kela
Joshua Kelley
Jim Kelly
Matt Kemp
Derek Kennard
Tom Kennedy
Shiloh Keo
Rex Kern
Steve Kerr
Tyrone Keys
Edward King
Jason King
Akeem King
Terry Kirby
Christian Kirksey

ABOVE THE LAW

George Kittle
Sammy Knight
Kris Kocurek
Bill Kollar
Steve Korte
Chris Kuper
Matt LaCosse
Anthony
  Lamando
Josh Lambo
Kendall Lamm
Jake Lampman
Loren Landow
Jarvis Landry
Eric Lane
Cedrick Lang
Jesse Langvardt
Matt Lawrence
Nate Lawrie
Emanuel Lawson
Vonta Leach
Kari Lee
James Lee
Cleo Lemon
Laveranues Leon
  Coles Jr. Darius
  Leonard
Fred Lester
Jerry Levias
DeAndre Levy
Tyquan Lewis
Thomas Lewis
Jermaine Lewis
Jeremy Lincoln
Adam Linger
Chris Long
David Long
Shed Long
Jammal Lord
Clarence Love
Jordan Lucas
Cornelius Lucus
Sean Lumpkin
Cameron Lynch
Aaron Lynch
Marlon Mack
Jordan Mack
Mark Maddox
Sam Madison
Mike Mallory

Doug Marrone
Leonard Marshall
Koda Martin
Jason Martin
Chris Martin
Gabe Martin
Eric Martin Jr.
Glenn Martinez
Robert Mathis
Ross Matiscik
Chris Matthews
Alexander
  Mattison
Brett Maxie
Marcus Maxwell
Ray May
Cameron Maybin
Baker Mayfield
Corey Mays
Joey Mbu Jr.
Ben McAdoo
Deuce McAllister
Keenan McCardell
Reggie McClain
Devin McCourty
Jason McCourty
Josh McCown
Lerentee McCray
Marlon McCree
Andrew
  McCutchen
  Randall
  McDaniel
KC McDermott
Tyler McDonald
O.J. McDuffie
Leon McFadden
Kimario
  McFadden
Booger McFarland
Tony McGee
Kevin McGill
Michael McGruder
Guy McIntyre
Doug McKenney
  Benardrick
  McKinney James
  McKnight
Rodney McLeod
Tom McMahon

Brandon
  McManus
Erik McMillan
Mark McMillan
Sean McNanie
Tony McRae
Montrel Meander
Dave Merritt
Jason Michael
Arthur Michalik
Doug Middleton
Jamir Miller
Billy Miller
Rolan Milligan
Eugene Milton
Jonathan Mincey
Gardner Minshew
  Terrance Mitchell
Stump Mitchell
Earl Mitchell
Arthur Moats
Curtis Modkins
Ty Montgomery
DJ Montgomery
Kenny Moore
Skai Moore
DJ Moore
Lance Moore
Nat Moore
Jordan Moore
Marlon Moore
Emery Moorehead
Patrick Morris
Michael Morton
Raheem Mostert
Jamie Mueller
Al-Quadin
  Muhammad
Muhsin
  Muhammad
Bill Munson
Louis Murphy Jr.
Chris Myers
Picasso Nelson
Quenton Nelson
Corey Nelson
Shane Nelson
Steven Nelson
Ty Neske
Ryan Neufeld

PLAYERS COALITION LETTER

Anthony Newman
Tyler Newsome
Nathaniel Newton Jr.
Parry Nickerson
Steven Nielsen
Roosevelt Nix
Jeff Nixon
David Njoku
Derrick Nnadi
Josh Norman
Moran Norris
Storm Norton
Carter O'Donnell
Cornelius O'Donoghue
Anthony Oakley
Stephen Odom
George Odum
Marques Ogden
Larry Ogunjobi
Michael Ojemudia
Alex Okafor
Bobby Okereke
Ogbonnia Okoronkwo
Deji Olatoye
Josh Oliver
Louis Oliver
Donovan Olumba
Glendora Stephans-Wright on behalf of Gordon Arnold Wright
Kenny Onatolu
Joseph Orduna
Raheem Orr Sr.
Matt Orzech
Jerry Ostroski
James Owens
Devine Ozigbo
John Pagano
Ervin Parker
Glenn Parker
J'Vonne Parker
Riddick Parker
J'Vonne Parker
Ron Parker
Zach Pascal

Dezmon Patmon
Tim Patrick
Javon Patterson
Shea Patterson
Mark Pattison
Spencer Paysinger
Brashad Peerman
Mike Pennel Jr.
Donovan Peoples-Jones Breshad Perriman
Corey Peters
Tyrell Peters
Adrian Peterson
Patrick Peterson
Drew Petzing
Adrian Phillips
Shaun Phillips
Danny Pinter
Trey Pipkins
Michael Pittman
Lafayette Pitts
Chester Pitts
Anthony Pleasant
Austen Pleasants
Shawn Poindexter
Bill Polian
DaShon Polk
Marcus Pollard
Ryan Pope
Gregg Popovich
Jackson Porter
Daryl Porter
John Potter
Jerrell Powe
Dak Prescott
Peerless Price
Eric Price
Brian Price
Sheldon Price
Malcolm Pridgeon
Pierson Prioleau
Ricky Proehl
Mike Purcell
Anthony Q. Newman Patrick Queen
Glover Quin

Randy R. Beverly, Sr. Eason Ramson
John Randle
Thomas Randolph
Kenyon Rasheed
Keith Reaser
CJ Reavis
Jason Rebrovich
Silas Redd
Cory Redding
JJ Redick
Sheldrick Redwine
Travis Reed
JR Reed
Malik Reed
Ed Reed
Brooks Reed
Frank Reich
Chris Reis
Tutan Reyes
Ed Reynolds
Ricky Reynolds
LaRoy Reynolds
Luke Rhodes
Alan Ricard
Ray Rice
Quentin Richardson
Wally Richardson
Jeffrey Richardson Sr.
Elston Ridge
Charles L. Riggins
Victor Riley
Elijah Riley
Bill Ring
Derek Rivers
Derick Roberson
Cordell Roberson
Walter Robert Briggs
Craig Robertson
Rob Robertson
Eugene Robinson
Mark Robinson
Matt Robinson
James Robinson
Isaiah Rodgers
Jake Rogers

ABOVE THE LAW

Charles Romes
Carlos Rosado
Marvelle Ross
Tyson Ross
Lee Rouson
Dontavius Russell
  KeiVarae Russell
Mike Rutenberg
Donald Rutledge
Sean Ryan
Demeco Ryans
CC Sabathia
Nate Salley
Rigo Sanchez
Lonnie Sanders
Lucius Sanford
Rick Sanford
Mohamed Sanu
Ricky Sapp
Eric Saubert
Cedric Saunders
Joe Schobert
Dalton Schoen
Josh Schuler
Tony Scott
Josiah Scott
Trent Scott
Boston Scott
Chris Scott
George Selvie Jr.
Andrew Sendejo
Jordan Senn
Wasswa
  Serwanga
Isaac Seumalo
Scott Shanle
Rickie Shaw
Justice Sheffield
Derrick Shelby
Jeremy Shockey
Brandon Short
Cecil Shorts III
Kurt Shultz
Ricky Siglar
Brandon Siler
Mark Simmons
Justin Simmons
Jalen Simmons
Ryan Sims
Keith Sims

Alshermond
  Singleton Nick
  Sirianni
Matthew Slater
Connor Slomka
Greg Slough
Bobby Slowik
Scott Slutzker
Torrey Smith
Rod Smith
Emmitt Smith
Braden Smith
Bruce Smith
Derek Smith
Keith Smith
Shaun Smith
Alex Smith
Evan Smith
Wade Smith
Kahani Smith
Cedric Smith
Dwight Smith
Ito Smith
Keith Smith
Will Smith
Sherman Smith
Reginald Smith II
Reginald L. Smith
  II
Steve Smith Sr.
Ray Snell
Katie Sowers
Denard Span
Tony Sparano
EJ Speed
Akeem Spence
Noah Spence
Charles Spencer
Takeo Spikes
Greg Spires
Erik Spolestra
John St. Clair
Dave Stalls
Donté Stallworth
Josh Stamer
Johnny Stanton
Giancarlo Stanton
Kevin Stefanski
Jan Stenerud

Simon Stepaniak
Dominique
  Stevenson
Grover Stewart
Jonathan Stewart
Christian
  Stewart
Jarrett Stidham
Otto Stowe
Chris Strausser
Derek Strozier
Dwayne Stukes
Shafer Suggs
Pat Surtain
Harry Swayne
Harry Sydney III
Quinn Sypniewski
Dave Szott
Roger T Duffy
Steve Tannen
Jaquiski Tartt
Steve Tasker
Jonathan Taylor
Billy Taylor
Fred Taylor
Chris Taylor
Jawann Taylor
Davion Taylor
Patrick Taylor
Jamar Taylor
Quinton Teal
Marvell Tell
Wyatt Teller
Patrick Terrell
Keith Thibodeaux
Marcus Thigpen
Thurman Thomas
Adalius Thomas
Blair Thomas
Hollis Thomas
Tavierre Thomas
Joshua Thomas
Shaq Thomas
Chris Thompson
Billy Thompson
Chris Thompson
Lewis Tillman
Spencer Tillman
Jim Tolbert

PLAYERS COALITION LETTER

LaDainian Tomlinson
Cole Toner
Casey Toohill
Amani Toomer
Charles Torwudzo Jr.
Touki Toussiant
Jeremy Towns
Rodney Trafford
Lynden Trail
Drue Tranquill
JC Tretter
Justin Tuck
Baigeh Tucker
Casey Tucker
Cole Tucker
Jacob Tuioti-Mariner Fenuki Tupou
Kemoko Turay
Nate Turner
Derrek Tuszka
Courtney Upshaw
Stan Van Gundy
Phillip Vaughn
Wise Raymond "Bubba" Ventrone
Shane Vereen
Oliver Vernon
Jason Verrett
Lawrence Vickers
Jonathan Vilma
Troy Vincent Sr.
Andrew Vollert
Travis Vornkahl
Delanie Walker
Anthony Walker
Jeff Walker
Kenyatta Walker
Michael Walker
Tracy Walker
Al Wallace
Todd Walsh
Tim Walton
Denzel Ward
DeMarcus Ware
George Warhop

Kurt Warner
Damon Washington
Tony Washington
Todd Washington
Benjamin Watson
Brandon Watson
Josh Watson
Armani Watts
Trae Waynes
Fred Weary
Anthony Weaver
Jed Weaver
William Webb Jr.
Jason Webster
Jemile Weeks
Brandon Wellington
Dean Wells
Carson Wentz
Jeff Weston
Ja'Whaun Bentley
Phillip Wheeler
James White
Roddy White
Adrian White
James White
Aaron Whitecotton
Marcellus Wiley
David Wilkins II
Jim Wilks
Joejuan Williams
Chad Williams
Chris Williams
Aeneas Williams
Quincy Williams
Quinnen Williams
Shaun Williams
Calvin Williams
Lawrence Williams
Kevin Williams
Kobe Williams
Jordan Williams
Xavier Williams
Daryl Williams Jr.
Wally Williams Jr.

Mike Willie
Nathaniel Willingham Khari Willis
Jedrick Wills Jr.
George Wilson
CJ Wilson
Charles Wilson
Josh Wilson
Damien Wilson
James Wilson
Jamaine Winborne
Robert Windsor
Andrew Wingard
Ronnie Wingo
Chase Winovich
Blaise Winter
Mitchell Wishnowsky
Will Witherspoon
Will Wolford
Nathan Wonsley
Shawn Wooden
Al Woods
Robert Woods
Wesley Woodyard
Blidi Wreh-Wilson
Kenyatta Wright
Rodney Wright
Willie Wright
Brandon Wright
Tay Wright
Ellis Wyms
Isaiah Wynn
Milton Wynn
Rock Ya-Sin
James Yarbrough
Kenny Young
Usama Young
Trevor Young
Eric Young Jr.
Olamide Zaccheaus
David Zawatson
Raymond Zeller
Justin Zimmer
Jeremy Zuttah

In addition to the players and coaches, the following front office personnel and general managers have lent their support:

David A. Jenkins
Edward Aaron
  Perez
Christopher
  Acosta
Armond Aghanian
Robert Akinsanmi
David Akosim
Kelly Allen
Kahlil Allen
Leo Amos
Renie Anderson
Monique
  Anderson
Justin Anderson
Brock Anderson
Paul Andraos
Patrick Arthur
Nana-Yaw
  Asamoah
Chad Austin
  Jessop
Adrian Bailey
Chanelle Balfour
Chris Ballard
Lauren Bartomioli
Megan Bell
Nancy Bernstein
Andrew Berry
Lindsey Bethel
Heather Birdsall
Nicole Blake
Michael Blanchard
Dylan Bohanan
Steve Bohlson
Max Boigon
Allison Bojarski
Chloe Booher
Kevin Boothe
Stephen Bowen
Dustin Bowlin
Emma Bradford
Courtland Bragg

Alyse Brehm
Ron Brewer
Ethan Brodsky
Morocco Brown
Jade Burroughs
Joey Buskirk
Zach Byrne
Colton Cadarette
Lindsay Caine
Geneva Camacho
Lucas Cambra
Kaycee Canlas
Eddie Capobianco
Corey Casado
Nick Caserio
Dick Cass
Concetta Cavaleri
Gerardo Chapa
Jonathan Charles
Taylor Chavez
Hedy Chen
Mitch Chester
Kimberly
  Chexnayder
Hsu-Wei Chow
Louis Clark
Katherine Conklin
Daksha Cordova
Felipe Corral
Omar Coss Y
  Leon
Keith Cossrow
Kara Costa
Anthony
  Coughlan
Patrick Crawley
Matt Cummings
AJ Curry
Issiah Davis
Brian Decker
Alison DeGroot
Brittany Deise
Mike Derice

Amber Derrow
Keith Dobkowski
Anne Doepner
Gabrielle Doheny
Jordan Dolbin
William Dorrance
Anne Duffy
Deandra Duggans
Alex Duplessis
Philip Eident
Regis Eller
Joey Elliott
Rich Elmore
Hayley Elwood
Cameron
  Etheredge
Nicole Ewell
Amy Falkow
Hannah Farr
Carly Fasciglione
David Feldman
Eric Finkelstein
Gerverus Flagg
Matthew Forzese
McKenzie Fox
Lisa Friel
Zachary Galia
Robert Gallo
Belynda Gardner
Alex Gaskin
Logan Gerber
Amy Ghanbari
Cyrus Ghavi
Colleen Gilmartin
Richard Gitahi
Isaac Gittens
Tyler Glassman
Scott Goldman
Reaganne Goode
Colton Gordon
Jon Gottlieb
Ally Greifinger
Shannon Gross

PLAYERS COALITION LETTER

Amanda Guerriero
Lucretia Hallowell
Christopher
  Halpin
Jamie Han
Goldwyn Harper
Keenan Harrell
Sydney Harris
Chase Hartman
Mo Henry
Joanne
  Hernandez
Glen Herold
Candace Hickson
Henry Hodgson
Natara Holloway
Christina
  Hovestadt
Andrew Hoyle
Serena Huang
James Hubbard
Venessa
  Hutchinson
Stephanie Hwu
Kathleen Ikpi
Elizabeth Iniguez
Anthony Isetta
David Issiah
Arthur J. McAfee
  III
Boyd Jackson
Taylor James
Jacob Janower
Mike Jasinski
Maurice Jennings
Malik Jiffry
Janiece Jiminez
Peter
  John-Baptiste
Stephanie
  Johnson
JW Johnson
Matthew Joye
Tyler Judkins
Megan Julian
Ina Jung
Alix Kane
Hank Kauffman
Catherine Keenan
Liza Kellerman

Courtney Kelley
Kevin Kelly
Danielle Kennedy
Cassandra Kicak
Christine Kim
Nicole King
Emily Kinman
Kacey Knauf
Rachel Kohn
Scott
  Koppenhaver
Samantha
  Kordelski
Cara Kuei
Thomas Kurniady
Mike LaBianca
Jamaal LaFrance
Shirley Lalicker
Shannon Lane
Cady Langdon
Matt Lathrop
Jason Lavine
Patrick Lee
Damani Leech
Laura Lefton
Emily Leitner
Craig Lepire
George Li
Ben Liebenberg
Alissa Lieppman
Erin Littrell
David Lomeli
Lisa Loomis
Joseph Lovallo
Joe Lovallo
Michael Lujan
Brooklyn M.
  McDaniels
Fred Maas
Wayne Mackie
Wyndam
  Makowsky
Laura Malfy
Jon Marc Carrier
Dylan Marchionda
Dylan Marcionda
Josephine
  Martinez
Josephine
  Martínez

Jesse May
Michelle McKenna
Justen Medina
Marissa Melnick
Sana Merchant
Emily Michka
Allison Miner
Charlotte Minetti
Bryndon Minter
Douglas Mishkin
Mark Mitchell
Damon Mitchell
Anisha Mooradian
Jamie Moore
Jordan Morse
Brandon Murphy
Ryan Murphy
Jessica Murphy
Jaynie Murrell
Gabe Myers
Jacklyn N. Bove
Heather Nanberg
Gregory Nelson
Margaret Nelson
Gina Newell
Nam Nguyen
Rhett Nichols
Jarrett Nobles
Drew Norton
Georgia Nze
Denny O'Leary
Peter O'Reilly
Scott O'Malley
James Onumonu
Stephen P. Richer
Dennis Padua
Tasso Panopoulos
Nikki Patel
Aubrey Peacock
Marcos Perez
Andre Perez
Liliana Perez
Marcos Pérez
Les Pico
Kelsey Pietrangelo
Lindsay Pinckney
Tyler Pino
Bob Quinn
Brian Raab

ABOVE THE LAW

Joshua Rabenovets
Ashton Ramsburg
Sam Rapoport
Carmella Re-Sugiura
Matt Reamer
Amanda Remy
Ghazzal Rezvan
Yolanda Rivera
Tracie Rodburg
Jennifer Rojas
Isabelle Roy
Sam Rubinroit
Josh Rupprecht
Sean Ryan
Annely Salgado
Melissa Schiller
Sarah Schmidt
Josh Schuler
Grace Senko
Matthew Shapiro
Nick Shook
Shakish Simon
Russell Simon
Dajah Siplin
Carly Slivinski

Alexandra Smoczkiewicz
Jason Spanos
Donna Steele
Taylor Stern
Samantha Strejeck
Staci Strickland
James T. Collins Jr.
Sean Tabler
Mark Tamar
Allison Taylor
Jenner Tekancic
Kloi Terzian
Jordan Thomas
Dylan Thompson
Aja Thorpe
Nick Toney
Jamil Toure
Gina Tran
Kenlyn Tyree
Ted Tywang
Cory Undlin
Darren Urban
Victoria Valencia

Marcus van der Hoek
Kristen Vasquez
Christine Vicari
Allison Villafañe
Kelly Viseltear
David Wagner
Jarick Walker
Tanner Walters
Aubrey Walton
Cheyanne Warren-Diaz
Kirsten Watson
Ruth Wels
Devin White
Kiara Wilcox
Mollie Wilkie
Valeria Williams
Astasia Williams
Michael Woo
Rod Wood
Timothy Yoon
Darrel Young
Yasmin Youssef
Peyton Zeigler
Lucy Zhang
Marco Zucconi

ABOUT THE AUTHOR

Ben Cohen is the co-founder and former CEO of Ben & Jerry's Ice Cream. He is the founder of a variety of advocacy organizations and the author of several books, including *Ben & Jerry's Double Dip Capitalism: Lead with Your Values and Make Money Too; Values-Driven Business: How to Change the World, Make Money, and Have Fun;* and *Ben & Jerry's Homemade Ice Cream & Dessert Book.* Ben and his partner Jerry Greenfield are currently helping to lead The Campaign to End Qualified Immunity.

CPSIA information can be obtained
at www.ICGtesting.com
Printed in the USA
JSHW041752060521
14342JS00004B/5